Hawker Hunter

TONY BUTTLER

HISTORIC MILITARY AIRCRAFT SERIES, VOLUME 16

Title page image: Hunter FGA.9s of 208 Squadron, from Eastleigh, Kenya, formate near Mount Kilimanjaro. The right-hand aircraft, XE607, crashed during an open day at Khormaksar, Aden, on 29 March 1962. The subsequent report blamed a runaway tailplane trim fault for the accident. (Key)

Contents page image: North Weald was home to these 111 Squadron Hunter F.4s at the time of this photo, in 1956. (Key)

Published by Key Books
An imprint of Key Publishing Ltd
PO Box 100
Stamford
Lincs PE19 1XQ

www.keypublishing.com

Original edition published as Combat Machines No. 4
Hawker Hunter by Key Publishing Ltd © 2018

This edition © 2022

ISBN 978 1 80282 315 8

Typeset by SJmagic DESIGN SERVICES, India.

Contents

Chapter 1

Design and Development
Cold War Necessity

Development of the Hawker Hunter began in 1946 when the Air Staff raised a Specification and Operational Requirement, F.43/46 and OR.228, respectively, for a new day interceptor fighter designed to destroy high-speed, high-flying enemy bombers.

This new type would replace the wartime Gloster Meteor, but such was the speed of advance in aerodynamics, technology and weaponry during the late 1940s that by February 1948, the specification had to be updated and was renumbered F.3/48.

In the meantime, Hawker Aircraft's designers at Kingston, under Sydney Camm, had looked closely at what was needed to make an ideal interceptor. The team concentrated particularly on achieving the smallest possible frontal area with a single engine (some F.43/46 design proposals had two engines). This effort culminated in a design called the P.1067, and in fact, F.3/48 was essentially written around this Hawker project. Issued in October 1948, it called for a maximum speed of 547kts (630mph/1,014km/h) at 45,000ft (13,716m). The powerplant was to be a single Rolls-Royce Avon or Armstrong Siddeley Sapphire turbojet, while armament was to comprise two or four 30mm Aden cannon.

A beautiful Ministry of Supply study of a highly attractive aircraft – the first Hawker Hunter prototype, WB188. (Phil Butler)

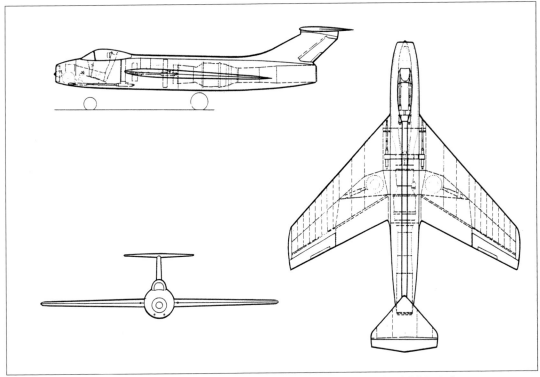

The Hawker P.1067 as it appeared in August 1948, when still sporting a nose intake. (Phil Butler)

Refinement

In August 1948 the P.1067 design had a tubular fuselage with a circular nose intake and a T-tail, the latter being considered the best from an aerodynamic perspective. In January 1949 it was agreed that the first two P.1067s should have an Avon engine with a Sapphire going in the third. Two months later, an ever-increasing equipment load meant that a nose air intake was no longer possible. This serious hurdle was solved by the introduction of a solid nose and a bifurcated wing root intake, an alteration cleared officially in January 1949. Apart from its T-tail, the P.1067 looked like a Hunter and as such, a part-complete full-size mock-up of this form was inspected officially in August. Finally, in October 1949, the tailplane was moved to the lower position on the fin, thus completing the Hunter's configuration as one of the most graceful aeroplanes ever built.

In addition to its wind tunnel research, Hawker had been accumulating valuable flight test data. The firm's first jet fighter was the straight wing and very successful naval Sea Hawk, first flown as the P.1040 in September 1947. Subsequently, two modified Sea Hawk airframes, serials VX272 and VX279, were completed with swept wings as P.1052s, so the manufacturer could garner first-hand experience of swept flying surfaces. VX272 first flew on 19 November 1948, but this pair retained the Sea Hawk's straight tailplane.

During May and June 1950 VX279 was rebuilt as the P.1081 with a new swept tail and all-through jet pipe, which gave a handsome layout of similar configuration to the Hunter but kept the Sea Hawk's more rounded body. Hawker Chief Test Pilot Sqn Ldr Trevor 'Wimpy' Wade took VX279 on its maiden flight in this new layout on 19 June 1950, and the aircraft was painted in a pale duck-egg green scheme characteristic of several Hawker prototypes of this period. Hawker's own P.1081 flight trials ended in February 1951 and the pilots reported how delighted they were with the aircraft. At its full fighter

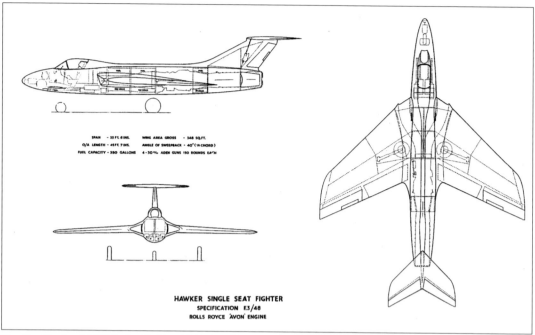

SPAN - 33 FT. 6 INS.　WING AREA GROSS - 348 SQ.FT.
O/A LENGTH - 45 FT. 7 INS.　ANGLE OF SWEEPBACK - 40° (¼ CHORD)
FUEL CAPACITY - 350 GALLONS　4 - 30% ADEN GUNS 150 ROUNDS EACH

HAWKER SINGLE SEAT FIGHTER
SPECIFICATION F.3/48
ROLLS ROYCE 'AVON' ENGINE

How the Hawker P.1067 looked in May 1949. A solid nose and root intakes were introduced but a T-tail was still present. This design was part-built as a full-size mock-up. Its span was 33ft 6in (10.2m), length 45ft 7in (13.9m) and wing area 348sq ft (32.36m²). (Tony Buttler)

weight, VX279 had displayed exceptional performance, virtually viceless handling characteristics, good manoeuvrability and a controllable Mach number up to at least 0.94.

In fact, it was considered superior to any other British aircraft then flying but, tragically, before official trials could begin, Wade lost his life and VX279 was destroyed in a flying accident on 3 April 1951. Wade and the P.1081 had, however, done much to confirm that the final layout chosen for the Hunter was good.

Hunter WB188 without guns fitted, before the aircraft's maiden flight. (Tony Buttler)

At this stage the P.1067 had no name. A British national newspaper contest had selected 'Demon', but the American Navy's new McDonnell F3H interceptor, flown in August 1951, had already taken this moniker and so 'Hunter' was picked instead, and announced officially to the public in March 1952. In October 1950, well before the first P.1067 had flown, a production order for 200 airframes was placed as part of an expansion programme for the RAF, brought about by the outbreak of war in Korea. The first versions were to be the F.1 powered by a Rolls-Royce Avon RA.7 and the F.2 with an Armstrong Siddeley Sapphire Sa.6.

Early flying

The two Avon-powered prototypes carried the serials WB188 and WB195, while the Sapphire-powered machine was serialled WB202. Hunter WB188, unarmed and again in duck-egg green, began taxi trials at the Aircraft and Armament Experimental Establishment (A&AEE) at Boscombe Down, on 8 July 1951. It made its debut flight from Boscombe on 20 July with Sqn Ldr Neville Duke in the cockpit, Duke having succeeded Wade as chief test pilot. In September he took WB188 to the Society of British Aircraft Constructors' show at Farnborough for its first public demonstration, where he recorded the highest speeds achieved thus far by any aircraft displayed at any Farnborough, and often just tens of feet above the runway. WB188 was then grounded between October 1951 and January 1952 for modifications to the fin and rudder, to try and stop vibration that had appeared as the flight speeds increased. Duke took the P.1067 through the 'sound barrier' for the first time in April 1952.

WB195 was the first prototype to have the four 30mm Aden gun pack and had its maiden flight on 5 May 1952. It was demonstrated in September 1952 at Farnborough and in December went to

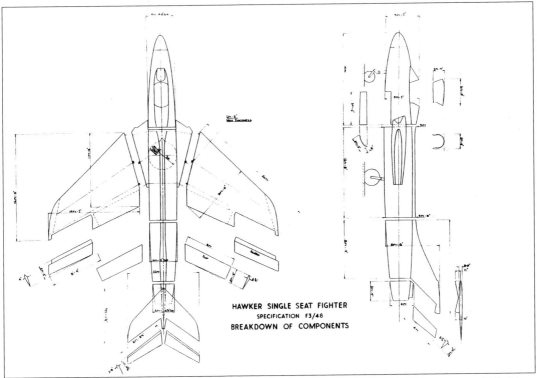

HAWKER SINGLE SEAT FIGHTER
SPECIFICATION F3/48
BREAKDOWN OF COMPONENTS

A drawing dated July 1949, showing the component breakdown for the T-tail version. For the Hunter as built this would have been quite similar. (National Archives)

Boscombe Down for appraisal. However, heavy vibration caused by elevator flutter was experienced when pulling out from a dive at low altitude and high speed, and WB195 then became involved in extended flutter trials to solve this problem; these lasted until December 1953.

In December 1952 work began on fitting WB188 with wing fuel tanks and a 9,500lb (42.2kN) thrust Avon RA.7R with reheat, as the sole Hunter Mk.3 (or sometimes F.3). It was repainted in a bright scarlet scheme and produced as a one-off for reheat development trials (to improve the rate of climb and acceleration) and as a test aircraft for the P.1083 supersonic Hunter described later. WB188's maiden flight in this form was made on 7 July 1953, but the powerplant provided insufficient improvement in level flight speed and Camm decided that reheat's extra weight, complexity and cost was not worthwhile. A higher thrust 'dry' engine would be better suited for the Hunter, which in due course appeared as the Series 200 Avon.

That said, on 7 September 1953, Duke used WB188 to set a new level flight world speed record of 727.6mph (1,170.7km/h). Although in almost all respects a standard airframe, WB188 then had a curved, highly raked fairing over the existing windscreen, and a pointed nose. The aircraft was based at Tangmere for the record attempt and the new figure was calculated as a mean of four separate speed runs, two in each direction, over a 3km course near Littlehampton in Sussex. A second speed record fell to Duke and WB188 on 19 September, the 100km closed circuit, which at the time did not

This photo of the Hawker P.1081 prototype shows its swept wing and tail and all-through jet pipe, features all employed on the Hunter. (Jo Ware)

For its early flights the first Hunter prototype had a spin recovery parachute housing positioned above the jet orifice, as visible here. (Phil Butler)

necessarily capture the popular imagination as did the air speed record, but for a fighter type for the RAF it was more significant. The recorded speed of 709.2mph (1,141.1km/h) was made in relatively poor weather conditions, around a course that started and ended at Hawker's Dunsfold airfield. It embraced a 25-mile (40.2km) straight outward leg, a 12-mile (19.3km) turn and then another 25-mile (40.2km) straight run home.

On retirement WB188 was used for ground instruction with serial 7154M and the prototype is now preserved, still in red, at the Tangmere Military Aviation Museum. Later in its career, WB195 was used for barrier trials and ground instruction with the serial 7284M and was not sold for scrap until 1967. The Sapphire-powered and silver-painted WB202 began its flying programme on 30 November 1952, and from mid-February 1953 was used for gun-firing trials. In March 1953, WB202 was fitted with an extended fin to provide improved stability, a successful modification applied to all subsequent Hunters. The aircraft was displayed at the 1954 SBAC Show, and in 1956 it took part in crash barrier trials, but was then used for firefighting practice and scrapped in 1960.

Development problems

Difficulties with firing the guns was one of the issues experienced during the programmes to clear the Hunter for service use. These were caused by surging in the Avon engine and came to light in late 1954. The powerplant would stall when the guns were fired at high altitude, though not every time. Early 100-series Avons had proved touchy when it came to surge because there was very little margin, and solving this critical problem took considerable time. However, a short-term solution was to 'dip' (reduce) the fuel supply just milliseconds before firing, which made a two-second burst at five-second intervals possible without surge.

However, the operational effectiveness of the Avon marks was not good enough; the Ministry of Supply (MoS) was not happy and Rolls-Royce designer Adrian Lombard met ministry chief Reginald Maudling to find something better. A further round of engine development followed, which lasted until the summer of 1956 and involved modifications to the Avon compressor. In addition, the Royal Aircraft Establishment (RAE) at Farnborough produced a modification that enabled the four guns

Neville Duke sits inside his bright red-painted record-breaking Hunter Mk.3. (Tony Buttler)

to be fired slightly out of synchronization, thereby reducing the effects of their blast (the blast of the four Aden cannon was so powerful it had damaged several nose components, such as the nosewheel rod, while another effect had been a nose-down pitch when the guns were fired at high altitude). These changes essentially cured the gun firing problem and modified engines were tested in Hunters WT573, WT574, WT612, WT736 and WV276. The later Hunter F.6 with 200-series Avon had a much-improved surge margin and never experienced any worries with gun operation.

Well before first flight, the MoS had warned Hawker of the need to ensure spent gun cartridges and links would have to be ejected clear of the aircraft. However, by July 1954, spent shell cases from firing trails were damaging the air brake because the deflector plates used thus far were just not effective enough. Hawker subsequently devised a scheme that employed two streamlined fairings fixed to the underside, beneath the cockpit, to collect the links and expended shells and these became a feature of production Hunters. The fairings were nicknamed 'Sabrinas', echoing the alias of a popular British glamour model of the period, Norma Ann Sykes.

The first two Hunter marks also suffered from a lack of fuel and endurance. This was addressed by two new Hunter versions, the Avon-powered F.4 and the Sapphire-equipped F.5, both of which carried more internal fuel and a drop tank beneath each wing. The fuel worry came into stark focus on 8 February 1956, when eight F.1s from the Day Fighter Leader School, at Norfolk's RAF West Raynham, took off for a combat exercise. The weather then closed in at their home base and the group had to recover to RAF Marham (in the same county) under ground radar control, but confusion ensued; the Hunter's landing approaches became stretched and just two of the fighters were able to land safely. The other six all crashed and tragically one of the pilots was killed. These early Hunters had run out of fuel after just 40–45mins.

The P.1067 Hunter was originally designed to also use its wing landing flaps for air or dive brakes. In November 1952, however, Sydney Camm reported that these airbrakes were proving ineffective at high speeds, while in the landing configuration they had caused large and possibly unacceptable changes of trim. Then in December the Hunter went to Boscombe Down for handling trials and the establishment's pilots found they did not like the airbrakes at all, declaring they were unacceptable.

WB202 comes into land, probably at Farnborough. Note the deployed flaps and undercarriage doors. (Tony Buttler)

Throughout 1953 and into 1954 the inadequacy of the Hunter airbrakes was another major problem, and in November 1953 the Air Staff stated that it would not accept the Hunter unless it was provided with effective airbrakes, which could be used safely throughout the aircraft's speed and Mach number range.

But it was not until February 1954 that the flap dive brake format was finally abandoned by Hawker, when at about the same time a new under-fuselage airbrake was produced. The airbrake trials, employing many available production aircraft, included the following two arrangements:

a) Fuselage brakes with the holes in the fuselage behind the brakes filled in, and with horizontal fins fitted to the top and bottom of the brakes, and to the fuselage opposite the brakes. The object of this modification was to negate the turbulence due to the holes in the fuselage, and to prevent the air flow from the brakes interfering with the tailplane.

b) A new type of rear fuselage brake fitted to an aircraft with a production-type jet pipe. These brakes were fitted lower down the sides of the fuselage.

Originally the fuselage brakes were designed to be fitted at the extreme aft fuselage near the jet pipe, but they were in fact installed on one of the prototype Hunters that had a jet pipe some 18in (45cm) shorter than on production machines, i.e., it was 18in nearer to the brakes. Flight trials in autumn 1953 revealed these brakes caused considerable buffet and an unacceptable nose-down change of trim, and this was thought to be due to the proximity of the jet efflux; Hawker subsequently moved the brakes approximately 1ft (30cm) further forward.

Fortunately, the decision taken shortly after mid-summer 1953 not to fit reheat to the Hunter made the addition of fuselage air brakes easier. An under-fuselage airbrake, which was considered acceptable by service pilots, was tested in February–March 1954, though in its original form it did not produce adequate deceleration and further development work was still required. Finally, after lengthy experimentation, the external 'barn door' underneath the rear fuselage became standard.

Hunter F.1 WT631 displays the prominent under-fuselage airbrake eventually fitted to all production Hunters. (Tony Buttler)

Hawker built the Hunter F.1s and F.4s, while Coventry-based Armstrong Whitworth was awarded contracts to produce F.2s and F.5s. Hunter production also became a subject of the British government's 'Superpriority' scheme, intended to improve the speed of production of several new fighters, bombers and other types. Following a rundown within the aircraft industry, with a loss of facilities and skilled labour, new types such as the Hunter and the V-Bombers, entering production at roughly the same time, had presented big problems with capacity and capability. Superpriority was intended to clear the bottlenecks, but in terms of a general acceleration of production it was only partially successful.

At one stage WB202 carried dummy de Havilland Firestreak air-to-air missiles. (Phil Butler)

Intensive trials

Hawker test pilot Frank Murphy took WT555, the first production F.1, on its maiden flight on 16 May 1953, and the first 20 F.1s were all used in various trials programmes. Between May and September 1954 three more F.1s undertook the type's intensive flying trials, but the first production mark fell short of the performance figures outlined by F.3/48, being very poor on time-to-height and ceiling (worse in fact than the Soviet Mikoyan MiG-15) and short on endurance and maximum speed. The Hawker Hunter F.1 received its Controller (Aircraft) C(A) Release to Service in July 1954, but with several limitations, including restrictions to gun firing, until the trials and modifications already described had been completed. Although falling short of F.3/48's requirements, because of its overall higher level of performance the Hunter had made a generally favourable impression and represented a considerable advance on previous British operational fighters.

A mid-1954 A&AEE review of the F.1 noted that for handling, the main attributes were generally docile transonic handling characteristics, excellent aileron control and a reasonably ergonomic cockpit layout. But at this stage these positive attributes were marred by the rapid pitch up in manoeuvres at high subsonic Mach numbers, and by the elevator becoming excessively heavy in that scenario. Trials with a fully powered elevator eventually brought considerable improvement in longitudinal control, and this was recommended as an interim solution.

WN888, the first production F.2 and the first Hunter from Armstrong Whitworth, initially flew from Baginton airfield near Coventry on 14 October 1953. In the cockpit was Armstrong Whitworth chief test pilot Eric Franklin, and superficially the Mks.1 and 2 were near identical. However, there was a small but clear distinction. Both had a small flush intake above the port side of the engine bay, but on the F.2 an oil-vent outlet was visible just forward of and below this point. Early F.2s were again used for trials and the F.2 C(A) Service Release was awarded in August 1954, but with similar restrictions to the F.1, though in general the Sapphire-powered machines had experienced fewer teething troubles than the Avon Hunters.

An official Ministry photo of the first production Hawker Hunter, serial WT555. (Phil Butler)

Chapter 2
British Operators
Variants in Service

The Hawker Hunter joined the RAF in 1954 and equipped many of the service's squadrons and a host of support units in the UK, in RAF Germany and in the Middle and Far East. Some Royal Navy squadrons also flew the aircraft and this section explores the Hunter's UK air arm service. Display flying, research activity and the Hunter's considerable involvement in various wars and conflicts overseas are described later.

Three F.1s from 43 Squadron – WT594/U (nearest), WT622/G (fitted with 'Sabrina' link collectors) and WT641/T. Note the unusual position of the rear fuselage code letters. (Crown Copyright)

F.1 and F.2

Trials and evaluation work kept busy the first 20 production F.1s. The debut RAF unit to be equipped with the F.1 was 43 Squadron at Leuchars, Fife. Its very first Hunter, WW599, was delivered from 5 Maintenance Unit at Kemble, Gloucestershire, on 29 July 1954, though 43's operational flying with the Hunter did not commence until mid-September as it gradually replaced its Gloster Meteor F.8 fighters. To begin with, the squadron's primary role was to perform intensive trials with its new mount, under operational conditions. For example, in January 1956 it carried out firing trials with new high-velocity 30mm ammunition, and in doing so the unit uncovered and/or confirmed the F.1's various weaknesses.

This sub-type did, however, display many worthy features. One was its short turn-round time after a sortie. In February 1955 the aviation press watched groundcrews remove the gun panels from one machine, detach the barrels of the four Aden guns, lower the huge gun pack onto a trolley before replacing the barrels, winch up a new fully re-armed pack (weighing 1,900lb/862kg), recharge the oxygen bottles, replace the gun's cine film, and finally complete the Hunter's refuelling in just 5mins 42secs.

In addition, the Hunter provided its pilots with substantially increased performance. Having struggled to intercept the Canberra bomber in practice for so long, they knew that such targets could no longer evade an attack. On top of this, in a transonic dive the Hunter could pass through into supersonic flight with considerable ease. A typical dive might start at around 40,000ft (12,192m) and it was possible for the pilot to aim his supersonic 'bang' at a chosen spot on the ground. The Hunter gave its first public demonstration of supersonic diving during a NATO air display held in Brussels, in July 1952, while on 30 November 1954, a German Parliament delegation visiting RAF Marham was treated to a spectacular performance. *Flight* magazine reported how:

> Two Hunter F.1s from CFE took off as a close pair and proceeded to give a most exhilarating performance. One of them started a battle climb to gain altitude for a sonic boom, while the other roared sharply skywards and disappeared from view. After a few minutes' pause, the commentator announced over the loudspeaker that the sonic boom was due, and that the aircraft might possibly appear before the sound was heard. This in fact happened. The Hunter raced silently across Marham at several thousand feet and had passed the aerodrome by the time a thunderous double-clap shook the tower, followed immediately by the howl of the aircraft's passing. A thick double vapour puff was visible at approximately 10,000ft (3,048m). The second Hunter passed by at 50ft (15m) at full power, only just preceded by its characteristic roar.

This was a sea-change from what had been possible with the Meteor.

A 263 Squadron F.2, serial WN946/N. (Brian Wallis via Roger Lindsay)

After 43's debut, the F.1 joined 54, 222 and 247 Squadrons and these home-based units were the only frontline examples to fly this mark, although airframes also joined 229 and 233 OCUs (the Operational Conversion Units that trained new pilots for Hunter squadrons) and the Day Fighter Leaders' School (part of the Central Fighter Establishment/CFE). The F.1's lack of range was ably demonstrated by CFE when, shortly after acquiring its Hunters, several took part in Exercise *Dividend*. Here the Hunter could for the first time fly simulated interceptions against fast jet bombers flying at high altitude (USAF B-47 Stratojets and B-45 Tornados, and RAF Canberras) and it proved successful in this role. Critically, however, no interceptions were possible at distances beyond 80 miles (129km) from base, a serious weakness in such an important task.

Just two squadrons flew the F.2, those being 257 (from September 1954) and 263, both again former Meteor operators. Further F.2s joined the Air Fighting Development Squadron (another CFE unit) during 1955, another (WN891) went to the Central Experimental and Proving Establishment (CEPE) in Canada for Hunter 'winterisation' testing, and two more were acquired temporarily by 1 Squadron. During their brief careers with the first two marks of Hunter, these squadrons also undertook a considerable amount of display and publicity flying, but by the close of 1956 the F.1 was no longer in the hands of any frontline unit, although some F.2s remained on strength until March 1957. Other examples of both marks were passed to training units or for ground instruction, but many went for scrap after very short lives.

F.4 and F.5

The first UK Fighter Command Squadron to re-equip with the longer-range F.4, from June 1955, was 111, which had been flying Meteor F.8s. It was quickly followed by 54 and 247 Squadrons, while the original Hunter units, 43, and 222 Squadron, had completed their conversion to F.4 fighters by March 1956. Finally, by April the Canadair CL.13 Sabres serving with 66 and 92 Squadrons were replaced by the Hunter F.4.

This Hunter F.4, WV269/H of 74 Squadron, lifts off from Horsham St Faith during 1957's Exercise *Vigilant*. Note the whitewash identity panel applied to the tail for these wargames. This aircraft was scrapped at 5 Maintenance Unit, RAF Kemble, in June 1961. (Key)

April 1955 also brought the arrival of the first Hunter F.5s, beginning with 263 Squadron. That May, 56 Squadron, which had previously been the only frontline unit to operate the early marks of the Hunter's direct rival, the Supermarine Swift, received its first F.5s. Other UK squadrons to convert to F.5s during 1955–56 were 1, 34, 41, 257 and 263, mostly as replacements for Meteors.

The extended endurance of the Hunter F.4 and 5 was shown to good effect very quickly during Fighter Command's annual Exercise *Beware*, held in late September 1955. This was an air defence exercise in which the participants would experience a simulated war situation. The Meteor F.8 had regularly been out-turned at height by the opposing Canberras, which could not only perform these evasion tactics but also follow up with quarter attacks on the Meteors themselves. The Hunters could now attack the Canberras from above, much to the delight and relief of their pilots! The aviation press reporting on *Beware* stressed 'that the new radar techniques and equipment, coupled with the indisputable success of the Hunter as an interceptor, have given Britain a vastly improved air defence'.

On 5 August 1955 Sqn Ldr Roger Topp, CO of 111 Squadron and who (as described later) would make his unit and its pilots famous for their display flying, flew a Hunter F.4 from Turnhouse, near Edinburgh, to Farnborough in Hampshire in just 29mins 33.4secs. This established a new (but unofficial) record and the average speed for the fight was around 680mph (1,094km/h). His achievement recalled, and was compared to, an effort made by an earlier Hawker product, a Hurricane, flying from Turnhouse to Northolt in 1938 (which took 48mins at an average of 409mph/658km/h); here was a graphic illustration of the advances made possible by jet power. Topp followed the feat a few days later with a second Turnhouse–Farnborough run, this time in just 27mins 46secs for an average of 717mph (1,154km/h).

September 1956 brought the next annual Fighter Command exercise, *Stronghold*, in which 41 (F.5) and 247 (F.4) Squadrons took part. The competition between the two versions revealed the Sapphire engine used by the F.5 gave that variant a distinct edge when it came to scramble times. During *Stronghold* the Hunters also tangled with Dutch F-100 Super Sabres, against which they performed

A very rare view of F.5 WN891, at the Central Experimental and Proving Establishment (CEPE), Rockcliff near Ottawa, or the Winter Experimental Establishment at Namao near Edmonton, both in Canada, during the type's 1955 'winterisation' trials. While there, WN891 was also displayed at the Namao Airshow. This aircraft never joined a squadron and was on the fire dump at Farnborough by 1959. (Key)

Hunter F.5 WP147 of 41 Squadron, which was based at Biggin Hill from 1955–58. (Key)

reasonably well, while the main targets were RAF Canberra and Valiant bombers and American B-47s. By autumn 1956 the Hunter had become fully established in RAF squadron service.

Although based in the UK, in 1956 1 and 34 Squadrons were detached to Nicosia, Cyprus, to permit their aircraft to take part in the Suez Campaign, and which for recognition purposes the Hunters had prominent black and yellow stripes painted around their wings and rear fuselages. Later, Hunter F.6s and FGA.9s would also visit the Middle East and this early detachment provided useful experience when preparing for later excursions.

One more squadron, 74, converted to the F.4 in March 1957, but from January 1958 this unit began to switch to the F.6. Again, both F.4 and F.5 were to spend a relatively short time on the UK's front line as the F.6 came on stream. The year 1957 brought 257 Squadron's disbandment in March, and the same fate befell 222 in October and 247 in December, while 34 and 41 Squadrons were disbanded in January 1958. No F.4s remained on Fighter Command's front line by February 1958, while the last F.5 unit, 1 Squadron, disbanded in June that year. No 56 Squadron continued to use a mix of F.5s and F.6s until November 1958, after which it became an all-F.6 outfit. No F.5s were ever based permanently outside the UK.

F.6

The F.6 with its later Avon 203 engine was clearly superior to the F.1–5 and became very popular with its pilots. The Hunter's airframe design meant the new engine could not provide the F.6 with a definite increase in maximum speed at all altitudes over what had been achieved in the F.4, but elements such as its rate of climb at height were vastly improved (at 45,000ft [13,716m] for example the F.4 figure was 1,000ft/min [305m/min], when the F.6 recorded 1,700ft/min [518m/min]).

The Avon 203's freedom from surging also eliminated the problems with gun firing at altitude; in June 1958 four 43 Squadron Hunters conducted an exercise where each F.6 fired all four guns twice at a height of 51,000ft (15,545m).

Unlike the English Electric Lightning's introduction in the early 1960s, when it would operate as an integrated all-weather weapons system, during the 1950s it was general Fighter Command policy to have two day fighter and one night fighter squadron forming a single wing at each operational airfield. The ascendance of Hunter F.6 squadrons was rapid, the first to acquire examples being 74 and, with a planned conversion rate of two squadrons per month, this unit was quickly followed by 19, 43, 54, 63, 65, 66, 74, 92, 111, 247 and 263 Squadrons; three of these, 19, 63 and 65, were still flying the Meteor F.8 rather than earlier Hunters. Non-operational RAF Hunter F.6 units included the Operational Conversion Units (229 and 233), CFE, the Fighter Weapons School, Central Flying School and Empire Test Pilots' School.

Although it was only capable of subsonic speed horizontally, the Hunter's rate of climb, agility and dive speed had enabled the fighter to intercept the British Canberra, and the American B-45 and B-47 bombers, with little trouble, all of which flew at heights between 35,000ft and 43,000ft (10,668m and 13,106m). This was important because similar frontline bomber types were currently in service with the Soviet Air Force, but the forthcoming RAF V-Bombers (Vulcan, Victor and Valiant) would be another matter altogether.

This straight-winged F.6, XF449/S, served with 19 and 92 Squadrons from 1957, and it received leading-edge extensions and gun blast deflectors retrospectively. (Crown Copyright)

Hunter F.6 XG164/H of 74 Squadron. Note the gun blast deflectors and the 'H' on the forward nosewheel door. (Crown Copyright)

This first became evident during a major NATO operation called Exercise *Strikeback*, a multinational and multi-air arm affair held in the north and mid-Atlantic over ten days in September 1957. For the Hunters involved, again the principal targets were Canberras and B-47s, against which they coped well, but the first of the V-Bombers, the Vickers Valiant, also took part and this aircraft's operational ceiling of 49,000ft (14,935m) gave it a valuable extra margin in which to evade the attacking fighters. Both Vulcan and Victor were expected to fly even higher and with even more performance, and the Avro bomber began to play its part in exercises towards the end of 1957. Because their mounts were only marginally faster at height than either Vulcan or Victor, Hunter pilots discovered that making a successful interception was especially difficult unless they could establish an advantage in both speed and height. This was a near-impossible situation because the first marks of both of these V-types had operational ceilings in the region of 55,000ft (16,764m).

Another improvement offered by the F.6 was its greater fuel capacity, which permitted Fighter Command squadrons from 1958 to undertake annual deployments to Malta and Cyprus for live firing practice over the less restricted Mediterranean ranges. The volume of air traffic in this region, both military and civil, also provided the opportunity for plenty of practice interceptions. As one squadron returned to the United Kingdom after completing an eastern Mediterranean deployment, it would at first land at the base of the next squadron to go out, so it could deliver the Hunter's outboard wing tanks, enabling the next unit's aircraft to make their ferry flights.

However, by this time it was clear the Hunter's day as a frontline interceptor was fast approaching the end and phasing out of the F.6, from premier Fighter Command units, commenced in 1960. Other reasons for this move were that several overseas air arms were acquiring supersonic fighters

Twin-seat Hunter T.7 XL609 was allocated to 56 Squadron and is pictured at Wethersfield in 1962. (Terry Panopalis collection)

One of the few occasions, indeed possibly the only time, when UK-based Hunters had to use weapons in anger. On 18 March 1967 the British Petroleum-operated tanker SS *Torrey Canyon* ran aground and broke up on Seven Stones Reef, between Cornwall and the Isles of Scilly. Fleet Air Arm and RAF aircraft employed bombs, rockets, napalm and kerosene to burn off the crude oil. Here, diving from top-left, a 1 Squadron Hunter drops napalm on the slick. (Key)

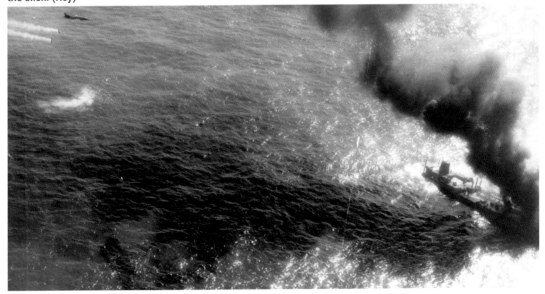

In the late 1950s T.7 trainer XL586 flew with 226 Operational Conversion Unit as 'RS/90'. (Crown Copyright)

that outclassed the subsonic Hunters (despite their heavy armament and excellent manoeuvrability), while the RAF itself had the new supersonic Lightning interceptor entering service. The Hunter could out-turn F-100 Super Sabres based in Europe, but with its supersonic performance the latter could certainly attack or disengage as it wished.

Selected Hunter squadrons would re-equip with the FGA.9 as ground-attack specialists, and some were to be based in the UK, but 74 began acquiring Lightnings during 1960 and flew both these and Hunters until the latter finally departed in November that year. Nos 56 and 111 converted to Lightnings in 1961, while 66 disbanded in September 1960 and 65 during 1961. Of the survivors,

A Hawker Hunter on the strength of the ETPS at Farnborough was F.6 XF375. It is seen here in 1966, being flown by Flt Lt Graham Williams. (Key)

While serving with the ETPS in the early 1960s, T.7 WV253 sported a nose instrumentation boom. The aircraft is pictured at Dunsfold. (Adrian Balch)

1 and 54 Squadrons came under the control of 38 Group, and 43 joined Near East Command based in Cyprus. Conversion from Hunters to Lightnings was undertaken by 19 Squadron from December 1962, but the last F.6 unit, 92, clung to its Hawker fighters until April 1963 when it too began to convert to the Lightning.

FGA.9

Tactical exercises had shown the F.6 to be a very good ground-support aircraft and this led the way for the modified FGA.9 'mud-moving' version (the Sapphire-powered Hunter F.5s did not have full ground-attack strength factors). Full conversion to the FGA.9 by 1 and 54 Squadrons took much of 1961. As such they became the offensive element of 38 Group as the Fighter Command Short-Range Strike Wing, though they remained available for air defence duties if required. But the primary task was to develop close support and co-operation tactics with the Army, and there were frequent exercises for this, for example, *Ringed Plover* in May 1961, which involved co-operation over the North Yorkshire Moors. No 8 Squadron also reformed on the FGA.9 from January 1960.

To illustrate how training and practice programmes were arranged, in January 1963 seven of 54 Squadron's Hunters flew to Bahrain for a month's deployment as a Strike Wing mobility and rapid deployment trial. May 1965 brought Exercise *Easter Lightning* in Scotland, where the wing provided support to an Army Brigade Group operating in counterinsurgency. Here the Hunters tried offensive operations against helicopters and defensive sorties in support of rotorcraft, but fast jets such as the Hunter were not really suited to such work. In June 1968 54 Squadron sent most of its aircraft to northern Norway for Exercise *Polar Express*.

F.6 XE601 was progressively brought up to FGA.9 standard, but never designated as such. It was used by the A&AEE at Boscombe Down for research (including biological warfare trials involving special tanks to spray water mist in simulated 'attacks') and with ETPS. This is it's later 'raspberry ripple' paint scheme. (Key)

Royal Navy GA.11 XE680 789/BY, of the HMS Goldcrest Training Flight (RNAS Brawdy) in December 1970. The scheme is Extra Dark Sea Grey over white, with Day-Glo panels on the spine, wingtips and nose. (Fred Motley)

WW664/699/LM was the T.8B prototype, but here wears 764 Naval Air Squadron (NAS) markings at Lossiemouth on 19 July 1969. (the late Jim Halley, *Air-Britain*)

During the second half of the 1960s the training programme included Hunter detachments to armament practice camps at El Adem, Gibraltar or Gütersloh (West Germany), where the aircraft fired or dropped SNEB rockets or bombs and/or cannon. The Short-Range Strike Wing's final practice camp with the Hunter was at El Adem in March 1969; 54 Squadron then disbanded in September 1969, while in July that year No 1 Squadron began to re-equip with the Harrier.

For a short period in the 1970s two other UK-based units flew the FGA.9, 45 Squadron from August 1972 and 58 Squadron from August 1973. This was, however, a temporary measure to provide operational ground-attack experience for aircrew earmarked to fly the then new SEPECAT Jaguar, and this Hunter Wing was disbanded in July 1976. In September 1974 229 OCU became the Strike Command Tactical Weapons Unit (TWU) comprising 63, 79 and 234 'Shadow' Squadrons. The TWU had some 60 Hunters on strength in four versions, the F.6 (but fitted with a Mk.9 rear fuselage along with its brake parachute), a hybrid F.6A (with the FGA.9's stronger wings attached to an F.6 fuselage), T.7 two-seat trainers (see later) and the normal FGA.9s. A second interim TWU was formed in 1978.

RAF Hunter frontline service in general revolved around practice flying and training, both minor and major exercises for simulating real combat and war scenarios, and the interception of unidentified incoming aircraft – all to combat a threat that fortunately never reached the UK.

Senior service

Bought for weapons training, the Royal Navy's single-seat Hunter was designated GA.11 and its two-seater the T.8. The GA.11 joined 738 (Advanced Training) Squadron in June 1962 and also equipped 764 Squadron. In December 1972 the surviving naval Hunters passed to the control of the Fleet Requirements and Air Direction Unit (FRADU), whose pilots were under contract to Airwork

Services (and subsequently Flight Refuelling). FRADU's Hunters were used to make simulated attacks on warships as an aid to training radar and gun crews, and to calibrate their radars. Other tasks included, in 1982 prior to the departure of the Task Force that would repel Argentina's invasion of the Falklands, dissimilar air combat training against Sea Harriers. FRADU's Hunters were finally retired in May 1995.

2 TAF/RAF Germany

Deliveries of Hunter F.4s to the 2nd Tactical Air Force in Germany (from January 1959 RAF Germany) began in 1955, and its replacement by the F.6 began in early 1957. The large number of squadrons equipped with Hunters was organised into groups, wings and squadrons. Number 2 Group covered the airfields in northern West Germany and embraced 121 Wing at Gütersloh, 122 Wing at Jever, 124 Wing at Oldenburg and 125 Wing at Ahlhorn. Meanwhile 83 Group looked after the southern German airfields with 135 Wing at Brüggen and 138 Wing at Geilenkirchen.

The 1957 Defence White Paper disbanded many squadrons, while others switched to roles such as reconnaissance. Individually, 2 Squadron became the last unit to operate Hunters in Germany (until March 1971), 4 Squadron became the longest-serving operational Hunter unit within the RAF as a whole, and 14 Squadron (the final F.6 operator) became the RAF's longest-serving Hunter day fighter unit.

Fortunately, the RAF Hawker Hunters in Germany were never called upon to take part in a real conflict, but the close proximity of the East German and Warsaw Pact borders meant their training necessarily had to be intense and realistic.

The Hunter F.4's main role here was again that of air defence. It was critical to have interceptors in a permanent state of readiness, so each airfield had a two-aircraft 'Battle Flight' ready for immediate response to scramble within five minutes of any violation of the Air Defence Identification Zone on the

This F.4, XE665 seen in 1955–56, was flown by the wing leader at Jever, Germany, and as such was adorned with the markings of the four resident squadrons: 4, 93, 98 and 118. (Brian Sharman via Roger Lindsay)

XE530/A and XF417/B were Hunter F.6s serving with 26 Squadron out of Gütersloh when this slide was made in 1958–59. (John Merry)

F.4 WW658/O of 98 Squadron in June 1956. This aircraft was never converted/upgraded and was scrapped in 1964. (Key)

Hunter FR.10 XF458/W of 2 Squadron pictured in Germany, in the early 1960s.

East German border. Two more Hunters would then replace those that had been scrambled, and each squadron would provide its base's Battle Flight aircraft for a week on a rotational basis.

Regular high-level practice interceptions were made against friendly aircraft under the control of ground-based radar stations. RAF types encountered included Meteors, Venoms and Canberras, while from other NATO air arms the Canadian Sabre was especially a fairly even match for the Hunter. There was also a monthly war exercise between 2 and 83 Groups, with as many as 60 aircraft flying at once. And twice a year each squadron would have live gun-firing on detachment to the Armament Practice Station at RAF Sylt, firing against banner targets towed over the North Sea.

The 1957 White Paper also brought changes to defence strategy, which for the F.6 brought more emphasis towards air-to-ground sorties with regular practice over the ranges at Meppen, Strohen and Nordhorn. T.7 trainers arrived in 1959 and examples were attached to each squadron, to Hunter Station Flights, the Armament Practice Station at Sylt and 402 Weapons Training Squadron. When the single-seat Hunters were retired, the T.7s continued with other frontline units in Germany operating types such as the Buccaneer. The trainer departed RAF Germany in 1984.

By the late 1950s the arrival of new supersonic interceptors with advanced radars and guided missiles brought an end to the Hunter's air defence duties. The FGA.9 was never based in Germany, but deliveries of the FR.10 reconnaissance Hunter began in January 1961. The images collected at low level by the FR.10's cameras were used primarily by the British Army, and in large exercises this version proved superior to rival supersonic photo-recce types operated by other NATO air arms. The RAF also had Hunters in the Middle and Far East, where they were either involved in armed conflict or at least a potential war situation. Their careers are described later.

The RAF's 4 Squadron flew Hunter F.4s and F.6s before converting to the recce FR.10 in late 1961, at Gütersloh in Germany. This example, XE580/D, carries a full complement of underwing tanks.

ROYAL AIR FORCE AND ROYAL NAVY HAWKER HUNTER UNITS

(Note: Most operational RAF Squadrons had some T.7 two-seat trainers on strength)

F.1

43 Squadron – 8.54 to 8.56, Leuchars

54 Squadron – 2.55 to 9.55, Odiham

222 Squadron – 12.54 to 8.56, Leuchars

247 Squadron – 6.55 to 7.55, Odiham

43 and 222 Squadrons formed the Leuchars Wing, 54 and 247 the Odiham Wing.

Other Operators: 229 OCU (Chivenor), 233 OCU (Pembrey), Air Fighting Development Squadron (Wittering), Day Fighter Leaders' School (West Raynham), Fighter Weapons School (Leconfield, Driffield 10.57)

F.2

1 Squadron – two aircraft only 1955, Tangmere

257 Squadron – 9.54 to 3.57, Wattisham, Wymeswold (from 6.56), Wattisham (1.57)

263 Squadron – 2.55 to 8.56, Wattisham, Wymeswold (5.56)

257 and 263 formed the Wattisham Wing.

Other Operator: Air Fighting Development Squadron (Wittering)

F.4

3 Squadron – 6.56 to 6.57, Geilenkirchen, Germany

4 Squadron – 7.55 to 2.57, Jever, Germany

14 Squadron – 5.55 to 4.57, Oldenburg, Germany

20 Squadron – 11.55 to 6.57, Oldenburg

26 Squadron – 6.55 to 9.57, Oldenburg

43 Squadron – 3.56 to 12.56, Leuchars

54 Squadron – 8.55 to 1.57, Odiham

66 Squadron – 3.56 to 10.56, Linton-on-Ouse

67 Squadron – 1.56 to 5.57, Brüggen, Germany

71 Squadron – 4.56 to 5.57, Brüggen

74 Squadron – 3.57 to 1.58, Horsham St Faith

92 Squadron – 4.56 to 5.57, Linton-on-Ouse, Middleton St George (3.57)

93 Squadron – 1.56 to 4.57, Jever

98 Squadron – 4.55 to 7.57, Jever

111 Squadron – 6.55 to 11.56, North Weald

112 Squadron – 4.56 to 5.57, Brüggen

118 Squadron – 5.55 to 8.57, Jever

130 Squadron – 3.56 to 4.57, Brüggen

222 Squadron – 8.56 to 11.57, Leuchars

234 Squadron – 4.56 to 7.57, Geilenkirchen

245 Squadron – 3.57 to 6.57, Stradishall

247 Squadron – 5.55 to 3.57, Odiham

Other Operators: 229 OCU (Chivenor), Air Fighting Development Squadron (Wittering), Day Fighter Leaders' School (West Raynham), Fighter Weapons School (Leconfield, Driffield 10.57)

F.5

1 Squadron – 6.55 to 6.58, Tangmere

34 Squadron – 10.56 to 1.58, Tangmere

41 Squadron – 8.55 to 1.58, Biggin Hill

56 Squadron – 5.55 to 11.58, Waterbeach

208 Squadron – 1.58 to 2.58, Tangmere

257 Squadron – 7.55 to 3.57, Wattisham, Wymeswold (6.56), Wattisham (1.57)

263 Squadron – 4.55 to 8.56, Wattisham, Wymeswold (6.56)

1 and 34 formed the Tangmere Wing.

Other Operators: Air Fighting Development Squadron (Wittering)

F.6

1 Squadron – 7.58 to 6.60, Tangmere, Stradishall (7.58)

4 Squadron – 2.57 to 12.60, Jever

14 Squadron – 5.57 to 12.62, Oldenburg, Ahlhorn (9.57), Gütersloh (9.58)

19 Squadron – 10.56 to 11.62, Church Fenton, Leconfield (6.59)

20 Squadron – 5.57 to 12.60, Oldenburg, Ahlhorn (9.57), Gütersloh (9.58)

26 Squadron – 6.58 to 12.60, Ahlhorn, Gütersloh (9.58)

43 Squadron – 12.56 to 1960, Leuchars

54 Squadron – 1.57 to 3.60, Odiham, Stradishall (7.59)

56 Squadron – 11.58 to 1.61, Waterbeach, Wattisham (10.59)

63 Squadron – 11.56 to 10.58, Waterbeach

65 Squadron – 12.56 to 3.61, Duxford

66 Squadron – 10.56 to 9.60, Linton-on-Ouse, Acklington (2.57)

74 Squadron – 11.57 to 11.60, Horsham St. Faith, Coltishall (6.59)

92 Squadron – 2.57 to 4.63, Linton-on-Ouse, Middleton St George (3.57), Thornaby (9.57), Middleton St George (10.58), Leconfield (5.61)

93 Squadron – 3.57 to 12.60, Jever

111 Squadron – 11.56 to 4.61, North Weald, North Luffenham (2.58), Wattisham (6.58)

208 Squadron – 1.58 to 3.59, Tangmere, Nicosia (Cyprus 3.58)

247 Squadron – 3.57 to 12.57, Odiham

263 Squadron – 8.56 to 7.58, Wymeswold, Wattisham (1.57), Stradishall (8.57)

Other Operators 229 OCU (Chivenor), Air Fighting Development Squadron (Wittering, Coltishall from 9.69), Central Fighter Establishment (West Raynham), Central Flying School (Little Rissington), Day Fighter Leaders' School (West Raynham), Empire Test Pilots' School (ETPS at Farnborough), Fighter Weapons School (Leconfield, Driffield 10.57)

T.8 (Royal Navy)

700B NAS – 4.65 to 5.65, Lossiemouth

700Y NAS – 11.58 to 1.59, Yeovilton

700Z NAS – 5.61 to 12.62, Lossiemouth

736 NAS – 7.58 to 11.58, Lossiemouth

738 NAS – 6.62 to 5.70, Lossiemouth, Brawdy (1.64)

759 NAS – 7.63 to 12.69, Brawdy

764 NAS – 12.58 to 7.72, Lossiemouth

803 NAS – 5.60 to 7.60, Lossiemouth

899 NAS (T.8M) – 8.81 to 10.93, Yeovilton

FGA.9

1 Squadron – 3.60 to 7.69, Stradishall, Waterbeach (11.61), West Raynham (8.63)

4 Squadron – 9.69 to 3.70, West Raynham (on detachment)

8 Squadron – 1.60 to 12.67, Khormaksar

20 Squadron – 9.61 to 2.70, Tengah, Singapore

28 Squadron – 5.62 to 1.67, Kai Tak (Hong Kong)

43 Squadron – 1960 to 10.67, Leuchars, Nicosia (Cyprus, 6.61), Khormaksar (Aden, 3.63)

45 Squadron – 8.72 to 6.76, West Raynham, Wittering (9.72)

54 Squadron – 3.60 to 9.69, Stradishall, Waterbeach (11.61), West Raynham (8.63)

58 Squadron – 8.73 to 6.76, Wittering

208 Squadron – 3.60 to 9.71, Stradishall, Khormaksar (Aden 11.61), Muharraq (Bahrain 6.64)

Other Operators 229 OCU (Chivenor), 1 Tactical Weapons Unit (Brawdy)

FR.Mk.10

2 Squadron – 12.60 to 3.71, Jever, Gütersloh (9.61)

4 Squadron – 1.61 to 5.70, Jever, Gütersloh (9.61)

8 Squadron – 4.61 to 5.63 and 9.67 to 12.67, Khormaksar, Muharraq (9.67)

Other Operators 229 OCU (Chivenor)

1417 Flight 3.63 to 9.67 Khormaksar

GA.11 (Royal Navy)

738 NAS – 6.62 to 5.70, Lossiemouth, Brawdy (1.64)

764 NAS – 7.62 to 7.72, Lossiemouth

Hunter F.6 XE587 flew with RAE during 1956–57 and was used for tail parachute development. (Crown Copyright via Jo Ware)

Chapter 3

Single-Seaters
Alone in the Office

The first Hawker Hunter variants were the F.1, which was equipped with a Rolls-Royce Avon engine and the F.2, which had the same structure, armament and equipment but was powered by a R-R Sapphire unit. The first production orders presented problems for Hawker Aircraft, based in Kingston-upon-Thames, in finding sufficient manufacturing capacity, so to make room some Sea Hawk production was switched to Armstrong Whitworth. In fact, many 'Kingston' Hunters were completed at Langley (major sub-assemblies came from Kingston) with initial flight trials at Dunsfold. Series aircraft were subsequently produced by Hawker Aircraft (Blackpool) Ltd and, for overseas, by Fokker (who undertook much of the licence manufacture in Holland), Aviolanda and de Schelde, and by SABCA and Avions Fairey in (and for) Belgium.

As noted, the one-off Mk.3 was prototype WB188, refitted with reheat as a trials aircraft. The fuel shortage afflicting the first two marks was addressed by the F.4 and F.5, both of which benefited from

F.5 WN958 carrying bombs on the inner pylons and tanks on the outers. (Crown Copyright)

The definitive gun muzzle layout was displayed by Hunter F.6 XE618 at the 1958 Farnborough airshow. The aircraft was converted to FGA.9 standard two years later. (Key)

internal fuel inside bag-type tanks in the wings, the facility to carry a drop tank under each wing, plus Sabrina blisters under the nose to collect used ammunition links. The F.4's maiden flight took place on 20 October 1954, and the F.5's just a day earlier. The latter retained the Mk.2's Sapphire Mk.101 engine, although one example (serial WN955) performed flight trials with the up-rated 11,000lb (48.9kN) Sa.7.

A major advance was the P.1099 F.6, which introduced the more powerful Avon RA.28 and gave the Hunter improved performance overall. The prototype XF833, which incorporated the centre fuselage and nose from the abandoned P.1083 prototype WN470 (see later), first flew on 22 January 1954. The first production Mk.6 made its maiden flight on 23 May 1955, and later examples introduced a revised wing with four hardpoints and an extended leading edge with 'dogtooth'. Another change (and retrofitted to early production F.6s) was a fully powered elevator to improve the Hunter's pitch response during flight at high Mach numbers. Much later the F.6A appeared with a brake parachute and 230 gal (1,046 lit) drop tanks on the inboard pylons, specifically to permit sorties to be made from the RAF Brawdy base, where the available diversion airfields were some distance away.

The first Hawker Hunter F.1 was WT555. (Tony Buttler)

In detail

The Hunter had a strong but conventional all-metal light alloy structure, with the frames numbered from 1 to 63. Its semi-monocoque fuselage was built in three sections – the nose housing the cockpit, armament pack and nosewheel, the centre section with the integral wing root stubs, the engine mountings and the intake ducts, and then the rear (detachable) fuselage with a hinged, hydraulically controlled flap airbrake (which could only be posed retracted or to full extension) curved to conform to the underside of the rear fuselage, an integral fin base, removable jet pipe and tail cone. The single-seat fighter had a sliding canopy that could be jettisoned, a pressurised and air-conditioned cockpit and a Martin-Baker ejection seat.

Gun armament for all single-seat versions comprised four 30mm Aden cannon in the nose (two left-hand, two right-hand) each with either 100 or 150 rounds, the latter giving a total firing time of seven seconds. These were housed in a self-contained quick-change pack fitted in the nose underside and which could be winch-lowered for re-arming and servicing (the gun barrels remained fixed to the airframe). The Adens were operated in conjunction with an automatic gun-ranging radar in the forward fuselage, its scanner in the extreme nose under a laminated plastic radome, and a gyro gun sight. The engine was installed in the centre fuselage, and fed by air intakes in thickened wing-roots, while the exhaust went straight through to the end of the fuselage.

All flying surfaces were swept rearwards. The wing sported a symmetrical Hawker high-speed aerofoil section and was built around front and rear spars (with an undercarriage girder running diagonally between) and covered by heavy-gauge skin panels. Hydraulically operated split flaps were positioned between the fully powered ailerons, and the fuselage and the ailerons had plain spring feel.

In this pleasing study, groundcrew service a 65 Squadron Hunter F.6 at RAF Duxford in 1959. (Key)

Above and left: Hunter underside views. The first shows F.4 WV319 in 1955, in clean condition (except for the airbrake), and with the original wing. The second has F.6 XK151 with wing extensions, 'Sabrina' link collectors and underwing pylons. (Crown Copyright)

The F.6's later leading-edge 'dogtooth' extensions provided greater chord on the outer wings, and were formed from short plate ribs with a heavy-gauge sheet wrapped around them and then riveted onto the original wing skin. The Mk.6 wings had a pair of stores pylons on each side to allow the aircraft to carry two 1,000lb (454kg) bombs, practice bomb carriers or four 100 gal (455 lit) finless asbestos plastic phenolic fuel tanks, or any combination thereof. And a total of 24 rocket projectiles could also be attached outboard of the fuel tanks, 12 carried per side.

The cantilever variable incidence tailplane was built as a single piece, it was mounted on the fin and again used Hawker's symmetrical high-speed aerofoil section. The surface was swept 41.9° at quarter chord and there was an anti-buffet bullet fairing at the rear junction of the fin and tail. Both tailplane and fin were skinned in light alloy, the elevators were fully powered and the electrically operated tailplane was also used for trimming. The fin employed closely spaced ribs connected to front and rear spars, it was swept 47.5° at the quarter-chord line and the rudder

The single-seat Hunter's gun pack, with barrels attached. (Key)

A study of Hunter rear fuselage detail provided by F.1 WT565. (Tony Buttler)

had an aerodynamic tab. Retractable Dowty tricycle-type undercarriage had the main wheels raising inward into the wing roots with the fully castoring nosewheel retracting forward into the fuselage (self-centring as it did so).

The F.6 had a larger tailpipe, while the version's automatic fuel system permitted the pilot to bang open the throttle, then close it and then open it again without risk of flame-out. In addition, the Avon 203 replaced the cartridge starter of earlier marks with an isopropyl-nitrate starting system, which allowed the engine to be rotated to self-sustaining rpm far more quickly, thereby allowing the Hunter to scramble in a much shorter time.

Later versions

The F.6s converted to FGA.9 standard introduced a stronger wing, slightly more powerful Avon 207 engines, new mild steel 230-gal (1,046 lit) drop tanks on the inboard pylons, a 13ft 6in (4.11m)-diameter tail parachute, and a bobweight in the pitch control circuit to provide more stick force for ground-attack manoeuvres. The first converted 'prototype' FGA.9, XG135, flew on 3 July 1959 and altogether 128 Mk.6s were upgraded as Mk.9s. In February 1968 FGA.9s received new Sperry gun sights, which provided air-to-air and air-to-ground modes for firing SNEB rockets, rocket projectiles or the guns.

During the mid-1950s a trial installation involved a forward-facing camera fitted in the nose of an F.4, and this brought forth a new requirement in 1957 for a modified Mk.6 to join RAF Germany, fitted with three F95 cameras, a braking parachute and 230-gal inboard drop tanks. Thus, the prototype fighter-reconnaissance FR.10, XF429, a converted F.6 airframe, first flew in modified form on 7 November 1959. In all, 33 F.6s were rebuilt to this configuration.

The next single-seat conversions comprised a batch of 40 surplus ex-RAF F.4s adapted for advanced weapons training for the Royal Navy. The resulting shore-based GA.11s had their guns removed, were fitted with an airfield arrester hook beneath the rear fuselage and had provision for rocket launchers on wing pylons. A small number subsequently had a Harley light fitted in the nose, to help with visual tracking when they operated as target aircraft; as such they were re-designated PR.11s. The first GA.11 began its trials programme in April 1962. Hunter production ended in the 1960s, but as related later, refurbishments would keep the manufacturer busy.

Testing

There is insufficient room to present detailed accounts of the assessment and approval testing of the various Hunter versions, but the following provides a flavour. In 1954 the Air Fighting Development Unit, part of the CFE, performed tactical trials with Mk.1 and 2 aircraft for the interception of enemy bombers. From an aerobatic standpoint the Hunter F.1 was found to be light and responsive to the controls, and all standard aerobatic manoeuvres could be executed with ease, although a considerable amount of height could be gained or lost during manoeuvres in the looping plane. They were, however, not well suited to the low-level role because of the small amount of fuel carried. The equivalent testing of Mks.4 and 5 in July 1955, with their extra fuel, found that the increased weight had produced a slightly detrimental effect on the performance and they were inferior to the F.1 and F.2 in fighter v fighter combat, but this was considered acceptable in view of the extended range and endurance. However, both marks were still not really ideal for low-level work.

Tactical trials with the F.6 were made in October 1956 and the greater all-up weight and increased thrust had given a shorter take-off run, a reduced time to height, slight increase in maximum level speed, and faster acceleration/deceleration, but a penalty was that increased fuel consumption reduced the radius of action and ferry range. The F.6 could intercept a bomber flying at Mach 0.85 at 45,000ft (13,716m) and the improved time to height enabled interceptions to be made 24 miles (39km) further

The handsome Chinthe badge and green/yellow checkers mark this Hunter, WN915/T, as an F.2 of 257 Squadron, which flew the type from 1954–57. (Key)

The FR.10 prototype was XF429. Note the nose camera windows to the side and extreme front. (Key)

out over the Mks.4/5. Times to 40,000ft (12,192m) were: F.1 – 7mins 48secs; F.2 – 6mins 20secs; F.4 – 8mins 35secs; F.5 – 7mins 40secs; and F.6 – 6mins.

A Ministry document from March 1956 gave the equivalent maximum speeds for each of these marks at 45,000ft (13,716m) as 524kts (971km/h), 529kts (980km/h), 521kts (965km/h), 527kts (977km/h) and 532kts (986km/h).

The F.6 with the 'electric flying tail' (fully powered elevator) and the parallel extended leading edges gave a noticeably more pleasant take-off and lighter stick forces. Its capability in the high-altitude interceptor role was not affected by the addition of the leading-edge extensions, but these markedly reduced the tendency for pitch-up prevalent in earlier versions and provided more manoeuvrability for fighter v fighter combat at medium and low altitudes. The electric tail also provided a distinct improvement in longitudinal control at high Mach numbers. CFE added that the F.6 was a very satisfactory and stable rocket-firing platform. This trait, coupled with external fuel tanks, handling characteristics, speed and gun/rocket armament made the mark an excellent air support weapon, and would result in the FGA.9. The initial C(A) Release for the Mk.6 cleared it for service use in the interceptor role by day only, in temperate climates with a maximum take-off and flying weight of 17,500lb (7,938kg) and a maximum permissible speed (strength limitation) of 620kts (1,149km/h) Indicated Air Speed, except when firing the guns. Within this speed limit there was no barrier regarding Mach number.

The sleek lines of the Hawker Hunter are shown to great effect in this splendid manufacturer's view of GA.11 WV380 taken, it is thought, prior to delivery to the Royal Navy. The Mk.11 had the extended wing leading edges. (Tony Buttler)

Hunter FGA.9 XG207/R of 45 Squadron 'Flying Camels' about to land. The unit received its Hunters on reformation at RAF West Raynham in 1972, but it moved to Wittering almost immediately in its duties as a ground-attack training outfit, until it disbanded in 1976. (Tony Buttler)

Early production F.6 WW593 poses for the official cameraman. (Crown Copyright)

Chapter 4

Two-Seaters

For Instructional Purposes

Hawker's two-seater G-APUX was demonstrated at Farnborough in 1960, with large 350-gal (1,591 lit) external ferry tanks. These were produced by inserting two 3ft (0.91m) sections into standard 230-gal (1,046 lit) tanks. Each had a lateral bracing strut and was stressed to 7g for ground-attack sorties. Note the gun and link collector arrangement. (Hawker Aircraft)

The Hunter fighter's flying qualities were so good that it was no surprise Hawker would produce a two-seat version. Although the trainer variants did not win the orders one might have expected from UK air arms, they proved popular overseas. In addition, although the number of new-build airframes was quite small, the relatively simple replacement of the original cockpits with the two-seat form enabled the manufacturer to modify many obsolescent and redundant Mk.4 and Mk.6 airframes, which might otherwise have been discarded.

Hawker P.1101

Design studies for Hunter two-seater trainers began in 1953 under Hawker project number P.1101, and official Specification T.157D was raised to cover orders for the RAF. It was decided the single-seat airframe should remain unaltered rearwards of the front transport joint bulkhead, just forward of the wing-root

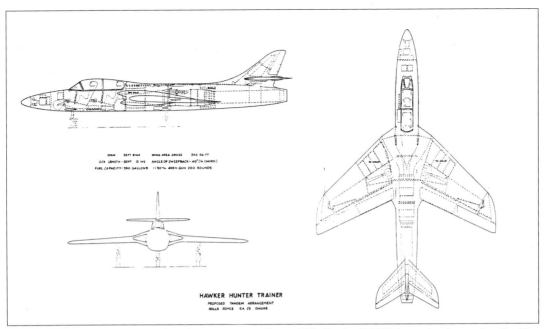

SPAN   35FT 8INS   WING AREA GROSS   340 SQ. FT
O/A LENGTH - 50FT O INS   ANGLE OF SWEEPBACK - 40° (¼ CHORD)
FUEL CAPACITY - 390 GALLONS   1 - 30mm ADEN GUN 200 ROUNDS

HAWKER HUNTER TRAINER
PROPOSED TANDEM ARRANGEMENT
ROLLS ROYCE RA 23 ENGINE

Drawings were prepared for a tandem-format two-seat Hunter. This Hawker P.1101 three-view for an aircraft with an RA.23 Avon engine does not carry a date. It had a span of 35ft 8in (10.87m), overall length 50ft (15.24m) and wing area 340sq ft (31.62m²). It carried one 30mm Aden in the port side forward fuselage, and 390 gal (1,773 lit) of fuel. (Hawker Aircraft)

intakes (i.e., identical to the Mk.4). The Hunter's modular construction made fitting a new nose reasonably easy and both tandem and side-by-side seating were considered, the latter because it was favoured for instrument flying and weapons training, while tandem seats proved best for advanced flying instruction. The tandem layout's weakness was that the necessary longer forward fuselage would require more vertical tail area, which in turn would increase the load on the rear fuselage, and so side-by-side was the choice.

The first of two prototypes, XJ615, made its first flight on 8 July 1955 piloted by Neville Duke. In the air, the original prototype cockpit shape, with its small fore-and-aft fairing, produced unacceptable turbulence and buffeting, and much noise over the canopy. An extended dorsal fairing only partly overcame these flaws, and the P.1101's handling characteristics were not perfect either. In early 1956 a wider and rather more bulbous fairing was introduced, which proved completely successful. There was some worry that this much fatter body, positioned ahead of the wing-root air intakes, might affect the engine and possibly cause flame-outs under certain conditions, but this proved not to be the case.

The new pressurised two-seat, side-by-side cockpit housed two lightweight Martin-Baker ejection seats and two standard fighter-type control columns. The cockpit also had two gun sights, but most of the equipment was concentrated in the left (pupil's) seat to essentially recreate a single-seat cockpit (with the single-seater's starboard console in the centre panel). On the right side the instructor had just a gun sight, altimeter, horizon, airspeed indicator and machmeter. Initially, XJ615 carried two 30mm Aden cannon in fixed ventral installations – quite different to the single-seater's replaceable four-cannon pack – but the port side weapon was removed later, and a blast deflector introduced to eliminate pitch and yaw when firing the starboard cannon. The new large canopy was heavy, and it was critical to ensure pilots did not get their arms in the way when it was closing. The solution was a horn that sounded continuously while the hood lowered, and it stopped only when the canopy was locked (signified by a small green light).

The first P.1101 prototype XJ615, pictured before a brake chute had been installed. A dark panel in front of the windscreen shows the limit of a temporary Perspex shield used to provide a smooth airflow over the hood. (Hawker Aircraft)

One of the T.8M conversions with Sea Harrier radar was serialled XL603. It sports 899 NAS's winged fist motif. (Key)

Despite the more bulbous forward fuselage, the trainer's compressibility drag-rise was delayed over the single seater; this balanced the larger surface area and so the F.4 and trainer showed no measurable difference in maximum level speed. XJ615 was powered by an F.4 standard 100-series Avon, and in April 1956 it began trials with a 10ft 6in (3.20m) diameter tail parachute to provide braking and reduce the landing run. This was housed in a fairing above the jet pipe, with the chute being anchored to the airframe.

The second two-seat prototype, XJ627, was quite different because it had a 9,950lb (44.22kN) Avon 200-series engine (making it an equivalent to the F.6) and the definitive forward fuselage from the start. Produced with the export market in mind, it first flew on 17 November 1956 and with the more powerful Avon, and delayed compressibility, it was marginally faster than the F.6. Hunter XJ627 had the drag parachute fairing, saw-tooth leading-edge extensions and a much more powerful horizontal tail control through the introduction of a fully powered elevator. The range of incidence for the tailplane was +31° to -2°. In essence this was an 'all-flying' tail and the aircraft's response at high Mach numbers, or during pronounced manoeuvring, was excellent. Coupled with the more powerful engine this made for a superior aircraft over the initial T.7/T.8 family.

Hawker Aircraft also acquired its own private two-seater, which served as a valuable demonstration/ development airframe. This Hunter carried the civil registration G-APUX and was designated Mk.66A. It was rebuilt using repaired component sections from two crashed Belgian F.6s, which were joined to a standard Indian Air Force Mk.66 cockpit that had previously been displayed at a Farnborough Show. It also sported two guns and an oversized braking parachute and made its maiden flight in this condition on 12 August 1959. Hawker Chief Test Pilot 'Bill' Bedford, Neville Duke's successor, flew G-APUX at Farnborough in 1959 and 1960, and during his displays he used smoke (created by injecting diesel oil into the exhaust) to demonstrate 12-turn erect spins starting from altitudes of approximately 15,000ft (4,572m). Recovery from a spin was straightforward, by centralising the control column against a white mark on the instrument panel. After having been test-flown by several air forces, in the process proving a major contribution to winning new orders (for example in 1959 it was leased to the Swiss Air Force), G-APUX was in 1966 converted to a T.72 with the serial J-718 for the Chilean Air Force. However, no T.66 variants joined British air arms, since sufficient F.4s were available for conversion to T.7/T.8 standard.

Singapore Air Force T.75 '500' at RAF Brawdy, Wales on 28 June 1976. (Key)

Royal Navy T.8 XF322 was converted from an F.4 and is seen here in the 1960s, as 962/HF of the Hal Far Test Flight, Malta. (Air-Britain)

T.7

The RAF's order for two-seat Hunters, designated T.7s, covered 55 new-build airframes, but in due course ten of these were switched to a Royal Navy T.8 order. A supplementary acquisition meant another 28 F.4s were converted to Mk.7 standard, which brought the RAF complement to 73. The Mk.7 equated to late-production F.4s, so the wing had provision for two outboard pylons and rocket pods plus eight sets of 3in (76.2mm) rocket projectiles. The first production machine was serial XL563, which first became airborne on 11 October 1957.

A 1959 study of a T.7 cockpit. Note the two heads-up displays. (Hawker Aircraft)

In early 1960 T.62 '681', ex-F.4 WT706, became the only two-seater acquired by Peru. The photo was taken at Hawker in autumn 1959 and the aircraft was delivered by sea. (Hawker Aircraft)

Hawker had hoped the RAF would select the T.7 as its new advanced trainer to replace the de Havilland Vampire, but the small and cheaper Folland Gnat was bought instead and so the T.7s were used for tactical weapons instruction, and to provide advanced flying training specifically for 'tall' students and for overseas pilots on attachment to the RAF. The first production deliveries, in August 1958, went to 229 OCU at Chivenor and frontline Hunter squadrons usually had one each. When the fighter was retired, surplus T.7s joined 4 Flying Training School at Valley. Four more were used for trials and one, XL574, was subsequently fatigue-tested to destruction. Three more flew with the Air Fighting Development School. A later sub-type was the T.7A, which was fitted with an Integrated Flight Instrumentation System (IFIS) to train and convert pilots to fly the English Electric Lightning interceptor and Blackburn Buccaneer strike aircraft.

T.8

The ten two-seat trainers diverted to the Royal Navy were designated T.8 and were supplemented by another 18 F.4 conversions. These were to be used to train de Havilland Sea Vixen and Supermarine Scimitar fighter pilots, and the main difference from the T.7 was the fitting of an arrestor hook. However, the T.8 was not stressed for carrier-capability and the hook was to be employed for practice landings on normal airfields. Rebuilt F.4 WW664 served as the T.8 prototype and first flew in this form on 3 March 1958. The first new-build T.8 was XL580, first flown on 30 May 1958, and deliveries began during the summer.

Later, to train Buccaneer pilots, four examples were modified as T.8Bs with a TACAN radio-navigation system and IFIS (both guns and ranging radar were removed). Eleven more were converted to T.8Cs with TACAN and some of these carried a Harley light in their noses. From 1979 there was the T.8M fitted with the Sea Harrier fighter's Blue Fox radar in a pointed nose. Three examples were upgraded as T.8Ms for training Sea Harrier pilots.

A beautiful study of WV363, a T.8 from 764 NAS, carrying rockets and practice bombs. (Key)

T.12

Finally, from the British perspective, there was the one-off T.12, serial XE531. This was a converted former F.6/FGA.9 with an Avon 203 and was delivered as a two-seater in February 1963. It carried no guns and was earmarked for service with RAE Farnborough and Bedford. In its nose was a trial installation of a large vertical survey camera, together with head-up displays (HUDs) in the cockpit to enable its pilots to perform trials for the forthcoming BAC TSR.2 strike aircraft. The latter's need to approach a target at low level beneath enemy radar, using terrain-following gear, had helped in the development of a head-up display, which was then very advanced equipment. On this Hunter, the camera fitting was visible in the form of a distinctive bulge on top of its nose to accommodate the equipment.

Extensive trials ensured more than 100 hours' flying were recorded by early September 1964, which proved the validity and effectiveness of the basic principle. At one point it seemed likely that further examples might be converted to a similar standard, to enable the Mk.12 to become a TSR.2 instrument trainer, but in 1965 the strike aircraft was cancelled and so XE531 remained the sole example.

The RAE's T.12 wore a vivid green and white colour scheme. This mid-1960s view shows the distinctive bulge on top of its nose to cover the camera fitting. A P.1127 V/STOL prototype sits in the distance, behind the nosewheel.

Nevertheless, these trials resulted in a useful accumulation of experience in advanced instrumentation. Afterwards RAE used XE531 for more research, for example with a fly-by-wire flight control system. It eventually lost the distinctive nose bulge, but the aircraft was lost in an accident in March 1982. This was the only UK-based two-seat Hunter with the powerful Avon Mk.203/207 powerplant.

Overseas orders

A multitude of nations bought two-seat Hunters, the 200-series especially serving either as a trainer or tactical aircraft. Some two-seat overseas orders were new-build airframes and are highlighted in this book's production list, but the deliveries detailed below were all conversions from retired F.4s or F.6s or, in some cases, acquired second-hand from other air arms.

Exports with the Avon 100-series were Abu Dhabi (2 x T.77s, serials 711 and 712 – ex Danish T.7s), Denmark (2 x T.53, serials ET-273 and ET-274 to supplement new-build), Kenya (2 x T.81, serials 801 and 802), Peru (1 x T.62 serial 681), Qatar (1 x T.79, QA-13, ex-Dutch), Saudi Arabia (2 x T.7, serials 70/616 and 70/617, ex-RAF), Singapore (4 x T.75, 500, 504, 514 and 516, and 5 x T.75A, 528, 532, 536, 540 and 544), Somalia (1 x T.77, CC-711 ex-Dutch) and Switzerland (8 x T.68, which had provision for carrying Sidewinder air-to-air missiles, J-4201 to J-4208).

India's two-seaters were based on the second P.1101, XJ627, with the more powerful engine and they had a second 30mm gun. This was the first order for the later trainer version and the 200-series Avon enabled higher take-off weights for India's hotter temperatures. There were 22 new-build T.66s plus 12 T.66Ds with two 230-gal (1,045 lit) drop tanks (serials S570 to S581) and 5 T.66Es with different avionics (S1389 to S1393). Other two-seaters fitted with the 200-series Avon went to Chile (7 x T.72, serials J-718–J-723 plus J-736), Iraq (5 x T.69, 567-569, 626 and 627), Jordan (1 x new build plus 3 x T.66B conversions, 714, 716, 718 and 722), Kuwait (5 x T.67, 210, 211 and 218–220), Lebanon (3 x T.66C, L-280 to L-282) and Oman (3 x T.66B and 2 x T.67, 800–804).

Like the single-seaters, the Hunter two-seat versions were all rather short of internal fuel, so had to carry external tanks to achieve a satisfactory range. But in service they proved hugely successful and in general had long service lives.

The Royal Netherlands Air Force was the only overseas air arm to operate all new-build two-seat Hunters, rather than converted airframes. This view shows 'N-304', which was first flown on 24 June 1958, by Hawker test pilot Frank Bullen. (Key)

Chapter 5

Test and Trials

Expanding the Envelope

Unlike other British aircraft such as the Gloster Meteor fighter and English Electric Canberra bomber (both of which had two engines and were well suited as engine test beds, and trials airframes for new avionics such as radars), the Hunter was not used extensively for general research programmes.

However, a number of single-seat airframes were adapted for experimental use, but in many cases purely for possible future developments of the basic airframe. The listing that follows is not exhaustive.

XF310, with two dummy Fairey Fireflash missiles and a nose-mounted ranging radar, was captured in this publicity photo prior to or during the 1956 Farnborough show. Note the absence of roundels and markings, due to the RAF not wanting any insignia shown because it still had not endorsed the weapon. (Tony Buttler)

Airframe

To begin with, one further change from the standard design was considered by Hawker. In February 1953 American sources quoted designer Sydney Camm as favouring external tanks 'snuggled up under the wings' on the Hunter, as opposed to wing tip tanks. Tip tanks had been assessed but appear to have been rejected, and that November's *Flight* magazine noted that 'reports of a Hunter flying with slipper tanks mounted on the undersides of the wings are incorrect; such a development has not yet been flown'. Then in September 1956 Hunter F.6 XG131 appeared at Farnborough (static only) with permanently attached, partly underslung metal tip tanks of 85 gal (386 lit) capacity, and which had finely faired sleeves over the normal wing tips; these tanks had navigation lights in their noses. In other respects XG131 was a standard F.6 and it first flew in this form on 16 August 1956, but unacceptable buffet was encountered (in fact possibly the highest level of buffet ever experienced by any Hunter). The aircraft apparently flew appallingly, this new arrangement ruining the Hunter's aerodynamics particularly at high incidence. Underwing tanks proved far better, and so no further work was undertaken on this project, which never received any Ministry backing. Hunter XG131 was subsequently restored to standard F.6 configuration.

As a brief illustration of the sort of research that was ongoing, especially during the mid-1950s, in July 1957 *Flight* magazine reported that three Hunters were with the RAE at Bedford. One had been mounted on a simple rig to determine moments-of-inertia in pitch, accurate measurements of the natural period of oscillation, together with data on the aircraft's weight and centre-of-gravity positions, yielding the required information. A second had been used to measure loads on the complete tailplane during in-flight manoeuvres, electrical strain-gauges recording the surface strain on the tailplane attachment fittings. A third measure was then employed to reduce transonic drag by introducing the 'area-rule' concept. Area-rule was best applied to the design of a new aeroplane right at the start, but it was felt that the drag of existing types could also be reduced by adding suitable fairings.

In 1955 F.1 WT571 had bulbous fairings attached to its rear fuselage, though in fact because of its shape the Hunter fuselage could never be truly area-ruled. After modification, WT571 returned to RAE Farnborough in early July 1955 to begin its flying programme, which lasted until October. The results indicated that just small increases in transonic performance

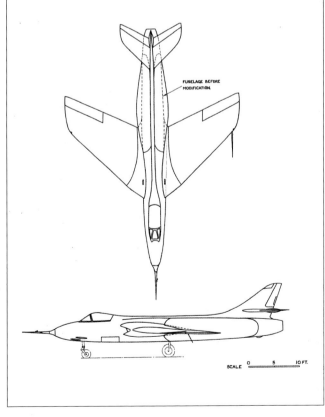

Drawing of Hawker Hunter F.1 WT571 with the rear fuselage 'area-rule' fairing.

A close up of XG131's tip tank fitting taken on 7 September 1956. The aircraft was mounted on jacks during the show. (Phil Butler)

had been achieved, though there was no increase in subsonic drag and a negligible change to WT571's handling characteristics. When flying in formation with another Hunter, the rear fairing had improved the maximum level-speed performance by about Mach 0.01 to 0.015. The fairing was not fitted to any other Hunter airframe and *Flight* reported that WT571 was later used to 'develop a technique of photographing shockwaves in flight, using direct sunlight as the illuminating source'.

From June to September 1955 RAE used another F.1, WT656, to assess Attinello blown flaps fitted in place of the Hunter's normal split trailing-edge flaps. This form of boundary layer control would enable the wing to develop increased lift at low airspeeds, primarily to reduce take-off and landing speeds/ distances. Boundary layer control took the form of supersonic blowing over the special Attinello plain flaps, air being bled from the Avon compressor and ducted to the wings, where it was ejected at supersonic speed through a slot 1.52mm wide, which extended over the flap's entire span. There was also a long nose pitot with a swivelling head to serve as the air speed indicator.

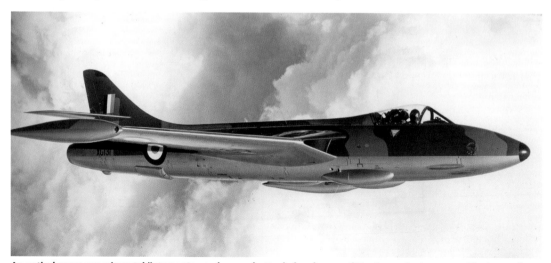

An entirely new experimental 'interceptor and ground-attack development' Hunter variant appeared in the static park at Farnborough, in 1956; XG131 fitted with tip tanks. This rare Hawker photo taken on 5 October of that year is one of the few to show it flying in this form. (Hawker Aircraft)

Above: Hunter WT656 with the Attinello flaps lowered. This aircraft also sported a nose probe. (Barry Jones)

Right: WT571 pictured at Farnborough, with the fairing attached to each side of its rear fuselage. (Barry Jones)

The flight test programme included general handling, measured take-offs, blown landings and stalls, and the results showed a reduction in stalling speed of between 1–10kts (1.9–18.5km/h), dependent on flap angle and engine rpm. However, this blown flap system for the Hunter had produced several new problems, including a strong nose-down pitch which, at low speeds, reduced the effectiveness of the elevator and tailplane. With blow operating there was also a reduction in engine thrust from 7,600lb to 6,700lb, restricting engine speeds on the approach. From the Hunter perspective, the only practical benefit of this system appeared to be the nose-down attitude, which improved the pilot's forward and downward view. From December 1957 WT656 was used for barrier trials and then from December 1959 was employed in noise tests at the Larkhill rocket-firing site.

Powerplants

In 1955 F.5 WN955 was fitted with an 11,000lb (48.9kN) thrust Sapphire Sa.7 200-series engine as a 'Mk.6 standby', which it is assumed was insurance against possible failure of the Avon 200 series F.6 development programme. The first flight with the Sa.7 installed was made on 9 February 1956. WN955 was painted silver and carried Class B mark 'G-1-2', but no photo has ever been found of the aircraft in Sa.7 configuration. From mid-July 1959 this Hunter was used by RAE's Radio Department for ground trials, which included running the engine to enable infrared measurements.

Possibly the most important trial concerning Hunter powerplants was the fitting of a Rolls-Royce thrust reverser to F.6 prototype XF833. This formed part of a general research programme for the Rolls-Royce Conway engine, which was to be fitted to forthcoming transatlantic airliners. When reverse thrust was selected, a pair of hemispherical eyelid shutters inside the Hunter's end fuselage would close, so that all of the RA.28's efflux was ejected through new lateral rectangular outlet grille exits in the rear fuselage sides, with multiple cascade vanes deflecting the exhaust outwards and forwards. XF833 was converted in mid-1956 and the work involved minimal external modification

The thrust reverser trials Hunter XF833 poses for publicity photos at the 1956 Farnborough show.

XF833's reverse-thrust grille. For the September 1956 Farnborough, the Hunter had a smoke generator in the tailpipe to show the direction of gas flow when landing.

to airframe or engine. Trials began in November 1956 and 308 landings had been recorded by April 1958. It was established that the landing roll distance with no reverse thrust and full braking was 2,520ft (768m), while the average with thrust reversing was an average of 919ft (280m) less.

Guided weapons

In 1956 Hunter F.4 XF310 was converted to carry two Fairey Fireflash beam-riding air-to-air missiles under its wings, suspended from the inner pylons on a spigot at the front, and a ball and socket bearer well aft under the wing. Beam-riding meant the pilot could 'fly' the weapon down a radio beam emitted by and aimed at the target by the launch aircraft. XF310's nose was extended and had an enlarged black dielectric nose cap radome to accommodate the beam-laying Mk.2 ranging radar. The four-gun armament stayed, but the camera port just aft of the radome was made deeper and longer, and normal pitot heads were mounted at both wing tips. In this form, XF310 first flew on 18 July 1956, and it displayed satisfactory handling characteristics.

For the 1956 Farnborough Show, XF310 carried no national markings and was painted blue underneath, with the two missiles adorned with what was described as 'a rather lurid colour'. Successful firing trials were completed in January 1957, and by September 1957's Farnborough, the dielectric nose cap had been replaced by an FR.10 nose with a vertical glass window, but no camera. Fireflash was not adopted by the RAF and XF310 was later converted to a T.7.

What is apparently the first photo to be released to the press of the Fireflash-armed Hunter. The date is given as 29 August 1956, although the aircraft appears to have its later Mk.10 nose.

Side-angle view of XF310 after RAF roundels had been applied. Fireflash had originally been codenamed Blue Sky. (Tony Buttler)

A much larger programme was an attempt to give the Hunter the capability to carry the de Havilland Firestreak infrared-homing air-to-air missile, which until 1957 was codenamed Blue Jay. Work began in 1953, but official Ministry support was cancelled in May 1956; however, Hawker elected to continue this effort as a private venture. With more engine thrust, the Firestreak radar/missile combination could be fitted to the standard subsonic Hunter without any loss of performance, and this would increase the fighter's interception capabilities, particularly at night. The new version was called the Hawker P.1109 and was a modified F.6 with (as planned) an 11,250lb (50.0kN) thrust Avon RA.24 (this in fact was never installed), a more pointed nose for an AI.Mk.20 air interception radar (codenamed Green Willow) and just two guns to reduce the nose weight. Otherwise the aircraft was largely a standard Mk.6 but it did not have the extended wing leading edges, and overall it was approximately 3ft (0.91m) longer. There was no intention to clear the P.1109 as a weapon system.

Three F.6s were selected for the trials, WW594, WW598 and XF378, although just XF378 received the complete conversion with radar, missiles and wing pylons to carry the latter. The first two were aerodynamic test beds – they had AI.20 radar installed and were known as P.1109As, while XF378

Close-up of one of XF310's Fireflash missiles (a dummy) at Farnborough in 1957. The store was launched towards its targets by booster rockets. (Key)

was designated P.1109B. The avionics work was undertaken by the Royal Radar Establishment (RRE) at Defford and both RAE Farnborough and Bedford's High Speed Flight were involved in the flying. WW594 first flew on 23 September 1955, and WW598 on 31 December that year. XF378 was first flown with two Blue Jays and its AI.20 nose radar on 12 September 1956, and in September 1957 it took part in the SBAC Farnborough Show (when the P.1109 configuration was shown for the first time in public).

WW594's take-off weight with its standard Avon 203 engine was 16,810lb (7,625kg), which included 150lb (68kg) of ballast to represent the radar. The highest recorded airspeed was 620kts (714mph/1,149km/h), the maximum recorded Mach number 1.16 (in a steep dive from 51,000ft/15,545m) and the greatest altitude achieved being 55,000ft (16,764m). The latter was reached in a zoom climb and is officially considered to be the highest altitude ever attained by any Hunter (although CFE test pilot 'Bob' Broad did get a brand-new and very light F.1, without its guns, to almost 57,000ft/17,374m). When test-flown in September 1956, XF378's all-up-weight with two 'uncharged' Blue Jays on the inboard pylons was 17,656lb (8,009kg).

In conclusion, the P.1109's flying characteristics and behaviour were considered normal for a Hunter, and overall the handling – even at transonic speeds – did not seem to have been appreciably affected by the nose extension, or by the presence of the missiles. In fact, XF378's general manoeuvring with two Blue Jays proved to be 'very satisfactory' and it could also be landed single-handed with one missile remaining, after one had been fired. Two Blue Jays were successfully launched from XF378 in early November 1956, but by the time of the September 1957 Farnborough show the Hunter/Blue Jay trials were almost finished. Just a few examples of AI.Mk.20 were built, all for trials purposes, and the equipment was never used operationally. WW594 was later converted to an FR.10, but WW598 was retained for use by RRE and RAE right through the 1960s, and still with its elongated nose.

At one stage Sapphire engine prototype WB202 had four dummy Firestreak air-to-air missiles loaded under the wings. Flight trials took place in May–June 1954 but were not connected with the later P.1109 programme. (Tony Buttler)

Hawker publicity photo of the Fireflash-armed P.1109B, XF378. (Hawker Aircraft)

There was to be another brief study into a Firestreak-armed Hunter, though. In July 1960 Hawker and de Havilland proposed a simple conversion, which would have the standard Hunter forward fuselage gunpack replaced by a similar self-contained pack with two Firestreaks attached to the sides of the lower forward fuselage. Two months later, however, it was clarified officially that two of the guns must be retained with the missiles and this killed the idea.

After completing its P.1109 role, WW598 was retained for further research with RAE. In due course it was painted in this attractive white colour scheme, and this view may have been taken at RAE's Llanbedr airfield in Wales. (Key)

One or two Hunters were used for trials work quite late in the type's career. This March 1976 photo shows an airframe engaged in air firings of an Air-to-Air Test Vehicle based on the design for a new Short Range Air-to-Air Missile (SRAAM), then currently under consideration by Hawker Siddeley Dynamics. The SRAAM twin launcher had been adapted to carry one round in the starboard launch tube, while the other carried instrumentation. These air launches were part of a technology development programme to prove, with a limited number of firings, that the predicted performance for the missile could be achieved. (Hawker Siddeley)

Above: The former P.1109 WW598 also flew in this bright blue colour scheme during its time at RAE Llanbedr. (A Pearcy)

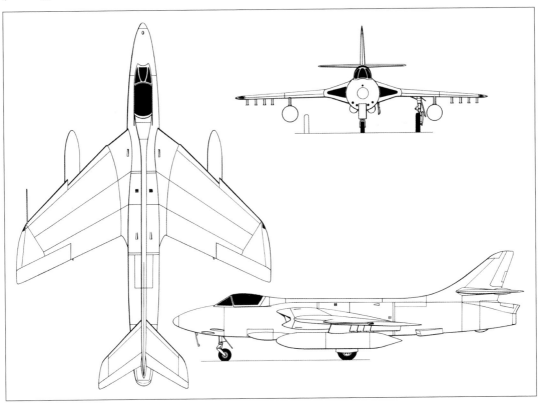

SPECIFICATIONS

Hawker Hunter Data

Type: Single-seat, single-engined, mid-wing cantilever monoplane interceptor fighter and ground-attack aircraft

Dimensions, all marks

Span: 33ft 8in (10.26m)

Length: 45ft 10 1/2in (13.98m)

Height: 13ft 2in (4.01m)

Gross wing area: 340sq ft (31.62m²); Mk.6 with extended leading edge 349sq ft (32.46m²)

Wing aspect ratio: 3.33

Wing thickness/chord ratio: 0.085

Tailplane span: 11ft 10in (3.62m)

Tailplane gross area with elevators: 53.9sq ft (5.01m²)

Tailplane thickness/chord ratio: 0.080

Wheel track: 14ft 9in (4.5m)

Powerplant

F.1: Rolls-Royce A.J.65 Avon (RA.7 rating) Mk.113 or 115 of 7,500lb (33.3kN) sea level static thrust

F.2 and F.5: Armstrong Siddeley Sapphire Mk.101 (Sa.6) of 8,000lb (35.6kN) sea level static thrust

F.3: A.J.65 Avon (RA.7R), 7,130lb (31.7kN) thrust dry, 9,600lb (42.7kN) with reheat

F.4: Avon AJ.65 (RA.7) Mk.113, 115, 119, 120 or 121, 7,500lb (33.3kN) thrust

F.6: Avon (RA.28) Mk.203, 10,000lb (44.4kN) thrust

FGA.9: Avon 207, 10,050lb (44.7kN)

Maximum internal fuel capacity Mks.4/5/6: 392 gal (1,782 lit) – front fuselage tank 200 gal (909 lit), rear 52 gal (236 lit), eight wing tanks totaling 140 gal (637 lit)

With two 100 gal (455 lit) drop tanks (F.4/5/6): 592 gal (2,692 lit)

With two 230 gal (1,046 lit) drop tanks (FGA.9/FR.10): 852 gal (3,874 lit)

With two 230 and two 100 gal drop tanks: 1,052 gal (4,783 lit)

Empty Weight: F.1 12,128lb (5,501kg), F.2 11,973lb (5,431kg), F.4 12,543lb (5,690kg), F.6 12,760lb (5,788kg)

Maximum loaded weight (clean): F.1 16,200lb (7,348kg), F.2 16,300lb (7,394kg), F.4 17,100lb (7,757kg), F.5 17,000lb (7,711kg), F.6 17,750lb (8,051kg)

Overload weight (1,052 gal/4,783 lit fuel): F.6 23,800lb (10,796kg)

Performance (F.6 clean)

Maximum Mach level flight: 0.95 at 36,000ft (10,973m)

Maximum Mach in a dive: 1.25 (in level flight, Hunter was incapable of supersonic speed but in a shallow dive went supersonic with ease)

Maximum speed at sea level: 621 kts (1,151km/h)

Service ceiling (rate of climb 500ft per min/152m per min): 50,000ft (15,240m)

Absolute ceiling: 52,500ft (16,002m)

Stalling speed in landing configuration: 105 kts (195km/h)

Radius of action (clean): 280nm (519km)

Radius of action (two 100 gal/455 lit drop tanks): 490nm (908km)

Ferry range (with 1,052 gal/4,783 lit fuel, landing reserves): 1,550nm (2,872km)

Chapter 6

Export and Overseas
Success Abroad

awker's factories built large numbers of Hunters for export, and further contracts were awarded to Belgian and Dutch manufacturers for licenced construction. Many ex-RAF and foreign-built airframes were also refurbished for sale around the world.

Abu Dhabi

The Abu Dhabi Army Air Wing received seven Hunter FGA.76s (ex-RAF F.4 variants refurbished to FGA.9 standard) in 1970 to equip one squadron. These were followed in 1971 by three FR.76As and a pair of two-seat T.77 trainers. Some single-seaters were then later transferred to Somalia in Africa.

An Abu Dhabi T.77, 711, in the 1960s. The camouflage was Dark Earth and Middle Stone over a vivid sky blue, with a red cheatline. (Tony Buttler)

Belgium

Belgium and Holland co-operated in a joint programme to build the Hunter under licence, the British fighter winning an evaluation against the Canadair Sabre and Dassault Mystère IVA. Avions Fairey and SABCA in Belgium, along with Fokker in the Netherlands, built F.4s and F.6s with their Rolls-Royce Avon engines manufactured by Fabrique Nationale at Herstal, Belgium. That country never acquired two-seaters because its pilots were trained in Holland.

The first Belgian-assembled example (ID-2) joined 7 Escadrille (Squadron) at Chièvres in August 1956; 7 Wing embraced 7, 8 and 9 Escadrilles, while 1 and 9 Wings (at Beauvechain and Bierset) commanded 349 and 350 Escadrilles, and 22 and 26 Escadrilles, respectively. Wings 1 and 9 lost their F.4s in 1958 and 1959 and 7 Wing's in 1960. In 1958 some SABCA-built F.4s were upgraded to partial F.6 standard but they could not take the Avon 200. The first F.6 was delivered in May 1957, and 7 and 9 Wings acquired examples from December and September 1957. No 9 Wing lost its Hunters in 1960 but 7 Wing kept them operational for ground-attack work. No 8 Squadron also served as a Hunter Operational Conversion Unit but was disbanded in August 1963, 7 Squadron following in November 1963. Belgian squadron codes were (7 Wing) '7J' for 7 Escadrille, 'OV' for 8 Escadrille and 'S2' for 9 Escadrille, and (9 Wing) 'IS' for 22 Escadrille and 'JE' for 26 Escadrille.

A Belgian Air Force F.6, coded IF-13. This aircraft was later converted to Indian F.56A serial A463. (Tony Buttler)

Belgian Air Force Hunter IF-61 'OV-W' of 8 Escadrille within 7 Wing, at Chièvres in 1960. (Key)

Chile

Between September 1966 and mid-1968 Chile received 15 FGA.71s (Mk.9 standard) converted by Hawker from ex-Belgian, Dutch and RAF F.6s. These were followed by three more FR.71As (FR.10 standard) and seven T.72s (second P.1101 standard). From 1970 a further 16 F.71s were acquired, all being ex-RAF F.4s/F.6s, and from 1982 another 15, although some of the latter were for spares only. Ground-attack and trainer versions flew with Grupo 8 and the reconnaissance Hunters joined Grupo 9, both based at Antofagasta.

The first Chilean two-seat T.72, J-718, in attractive four-tone camouflage. (Key)

This Chilean Air Force FGA.71 is loaded with practice bombs on its port outboard pylon, and a rocket pod on the equivalent pylon to starboard. It has also been fitted with chaff/flare dispensers on its rear fuselage. (Key)

Denmark

The Royal Danish Air Force had 30 standard F.4s delivered from Kingston as F.51s from November 1955. These all joined 724 Squadron (Esk-724) at Aalborg (later Karup and then Skrydstrup) and were followed in 1958 by two T.53s, with two more in 1967. No 724 Squadron did not disband until March 1974. Denmark's Hunters were initially finished in standard RAF colours, but they later appeared in overall green paint.

India

This large Asian country ordered 160 F.56s (F.6s), the first 32 of which were airframes earmarked for the RAF but cancelled while on the production line, and then cleared by the MoS for the new customer. The next 16 came directly from RAF stocks. India's first example was delivered in October 1957. All new-build F.56s had gun blast deflectors and tail parachutes, and some could carry 230 gal (1,046 lit) drop tanks. A further 22 T.66s followed with Avon 203s, the first being delivered in February 1959. Between 1966 and 1970 another 53 F.56As were supplied (Hawker refurbishments to Mk.9 standard from ex-Belgian and RAF), in 1966 also came 12 T.66Ds and in 1973, five T.66Es (all ex-F.6s).

The first unit to fly the Hunter was 7 Squadron at Ambala, which operated the F.56 from December 1957 to June 1973. This was followed by 14 and 20 Squadrons at Kalaikunda (both from 1958), 27 at Ambala (September 1958–1970s), 17 at Poona (from 1958) and 37 at Kalaikunda (from 1959). India's Hunter force was concentrated into two wings based at Ambala and Poona, each of which comprised three squadrons. Every unit also received two trainers and in addition an OCU at Ambala, comprising single and two-seat Hunters.

India's A484 was an F.56A, but when pictured here, near the end of that country's Hunter service, it was in use as a target-towing aircraft. (Tony Buttler)

Replacement of the type by the Jaguar in 14 Squadron began in 1979 and for 27 Squadron during 1985, but the process of phasing out the Hunter was very slow. Examples were retained for weapons training and as target tugs by 3 and 31 Squadrons within the Armament Training Wing based at Jamnagar. A Target Tug Flight was formed at Kalaikunda in 1972 and it was this unit that operated India's very last Hunters. A number of India's aircraft were lost in wars with Pakistan.

Iraq

Iraq initially purchased 15 Hunter F.6s from RAF stocks, paid for with American funding. The Arab nation's first Hunter squadron was duly formed at Habbaniya in spring 1958, and its pilots were trained by the RAF's 229 OCU in the UK. Another 46 former Belgian and Dutch F.6s were supplied by Hawker between 1964 and 1967, comprising 24 FGA.59s, 18 FGA.59As and four FGA.59Bs, and all were upgraded to Mk.9 standard. The two-seat element comprised Hawker's demonstration aircraft G-APUX on loan from 1963 (and later to Jordan and Lebanon), plus five T.69s, all ex-Belgian F.6s with new noses. Iraq's Hunters became involved in several wars over three decades. Serial numbers were painted on the rear fuselage in Arabic numerals.

An Iraqi F.59 shown at the start of its delivery flight from the UK in 1964. (Hawker Siddeley)

This Jordanian F.6 was photographed at Farnborough. (Tony Buttler)

Jordan

In 1958 the Royal Jordanian Air Force placed orders for 12 F.6s to equip 1 Squadron, which formed at Mafraq in November. These were all ex-RAF machines, as were another 12 FGA.9s (F.73s) acquired in 1962 to equip 2 Squadron, and two FR.10s in 1960. One F.6 and two more FGA.9s (all ex-RAF) arrived in 1967 and two more FGA.73s in 1968. No 6 Operational Conversion Unit flew single and two-seaters after a new-build T.66B (Avon 200) was supplied by Hawker in 1960, along with two more converted ex-Dutch F.6s. G-APUX also came on loan. Four F.73As arrived in 1969 (ex-RAF as full Mk.9s) with nine more following in 1971, along with three Mk.73Bs. Two ex-Saudi T.70s also joined the fleet in 1968. These later orders replaced war losses and the Hunter was finally retired from service in 1974. Some survivors went to Oman.

Kenya

In 1974 and early 1975 four FGA.80s (FGA.9) and a T.81, all refurbished RAF single-seaters, came to Kenya from Hawker Siddeley as a counter to then recently strengthened neighbouring air arms. A T.8C was acquired in 1973 and they were based at Nanyuki, but in 1981 the survivors were passed to Zimbabwe. Kenyan Hunters wore standard RAF Dark Green and Dark Sea Grey camouflage on their upper surfaces, with Light Aircraft Grey on the undersides.

A Kenyan Air Force Hunter at Luqa, Malta, in 1974. Note the large blade aerial behind the canopy. (Key)

Kuwaiti F.57 serial 212 at Dunsfold in 1965, just before delivery. (Hawker Siddeley)

Kuwait
Kuwait acquired a few Hunters in 1965–67 and another in 1969, with oilfield defence in mind. These comprised four FGA.57s (FGA.9 standard) converted by Kingston from Belgian and RAF F.6s, and one FGA.9, plus four T.67s converted from F.6s.

Lebanon
Israel's neighbour acquired five ex-RAF F.6s as FGA.70s in 1958, while in 1965–66 Kingston converted another four Belgian airframes to FGA.9 standard, still as Mk.70s. Another six ex-UK machines were refurbished as FGA.70As in 1975 and 1977. Three T.66Cs (Belgian F.6s) were delivered in 1965–66 and Lebanon also leased G-APUX in 1965.

Netherlands
Royal Netherlands Air Force Hunters were built under licence by Fokker and funded by the US government's Offshore Procurement Program (as were Belgium's Hunters). To begin, 96 F.4s were constructed with the first leaving the factory in February 1956, and the last in November 1957. Another 93 F.6s followed between October 1957–59, plus 20 T.7s from July 1958 – the first ten of the latter were home-built, with the rest coming from a cancelled RAF order. Dutch Hunters took part in major NATO exercises, they operated with NATO's Second Allied Tactical Air Force, and occasionally intercepted Soviet bombers. Belgian and Dutch pilots were jointly converted to type, using the latter's two-seaters (the reason why Belgium never bought trainers). Low flying training was also conducted at Goose Bay in Canada with RNethAF Hunters deploying there annually.

Six squadrons flew Hunters: 322 at Soesterberg had F.4s in 1958 only, with F.6s arriving from April 1958 and operating until April 1960. However, this unit re-equipped on the F.4 again in May 1960, when its fighters were taken by the aircraft carrier *Karel Doorman* to the island of Biak to provide air defence during the bitter Indonesian Confrontation in Dutch New Guinea. F.6s arrived in December 1961 and these could carry 230 gal (1,046 lit) tanks rather than the F.4's 100 gal (455 lit) capacity, although 322 Squadron flew both versions until September 1962.

A delightful air-to-air study of Royal Netherlands Air Force F.4 N-176, of 323 Squadron at Leeuwarden. (Key)

F.4s joined 323 Squadron at Leeuwarden in October 1957, when the unit's role was air-to-air gunnery training. Through 1959–60 they would tow banner targets until this task became the responsibility of the Flight Service Squadron. Further Hunters were allocated to a Conversion Flight, which joined 323 in late 1959. The latter's Hunters were withdrawn in 1963, while 324 Squadron flew the F.4 for a very short period because it was the first unit to switch to the F.6, in October 1957, flying that sub-type at Leeuwarden until 1964.

No 325 Squadron, also at Leeuwarden, was the first F.4 unit, from December 1955, and after moving to Soesterberg it received F.6s from September 1958. Next, 326 Squadron at Woensdrecht began conversion to the F.4 in November 1957. It switched to F.6s in 1960, having that year moved to Soesterberg, but was disbanded in December 1961. The F.4 also reached 327 Squadron at Volkel in 1957, but in January 1958 this unit was merged with 322 Squadron. The last operational F.4 flight was made in Holland in August 1963, and the last Dutch Air Force Hunter, a 325 Squadron aircraft, was retired in August 1968. However, T.7 N-320 became civil register PH-NLH to conduct research with the Lucht-en-Ruimtevaartlaboratorium (National Air and Space Laboratory). It was retired in January 1980.

Dutch Hunters used similar colours to RAF machines with Dark Sea Grey and Dark Green upper surfaces and High Speed Silver undersides. The T.7s were painted overall silver with Day-Glo areas on the nose, rear fuselage and wing tips. Initially, 322 Squadron used '3W' codes for each of its aircraft, 323 Squadron 'Y9' codes, 324 '3P' codes, 325 '4R' codes, 326 '9I' and 327 '7E' codes. The use of these devices lasted until late 1959, when they gradually began to disappear to be replaced by N-serial numbers.

Oman
The Sultanate of Oman Air Force received 40 Hunters of mixed variants, many coming from Jordan in 1975 but supplemented by examples from Kuwait and conversions from the UK. These were formed into 6 Squadron based at Thumrait, and the survivors were retired in August 1993.

Peru

Peru's Air Force ordered 16 F.52s (ex-RAF F.4s) and from 1956 these equipped one squadron within Grupo 12 (Escuadron de Caza 14) at Limatambo, and from 1957 Talara (other units within the Grupo flew American fighters). A single T.62 (ex-RAF F.4) was delivered in October 1959. Hunter flying abated from 1968 following a switch to ground-attack duties, but did not end completely until 1992.

Qatar

Three FGA.78s and one T.79, all ex-Dutch F.6s, and a T.7 were delivered to Qatar in December 1971, and were used until the 1980s.

Rhodesia/Zimbabwe

Rhodesia acquired 12 ex-RAF F.6s, updated to FGA.9 standard, between December 1962 and April 1963 to equip 1 Squadron at Thornhill. After independence, Zimbabwe bought four more FGA.9s and a T.7 from Kenya, and another nine Mk.9s came from Britain in 1984 and 1987. For security during anti-guerrilla operations, the air force changed the serials of many of its aircraft, and its Hunters carried random numbers in the 1xxx and 8xxx series. Rhodesian Hunters, and those of the Air Force of Zimbabwe, were given camouflage of Dark Green and Dark Earth.

Sultanate of Oman Air Force FGA.73B '841' as seen on 8 November 1980, in its effective low-visibility grey colour scheme. (Tony Buttler)

Saudi Arabia

Four refurbished ex-RAF F.6s and two T.7s were delivered to Saudi Arabia in 1966 to serve as lead-in aircraft to the complex and more powerful Lightning, ordered at the same time. The survivors were presented to Jordan in 1968.

Singapore

The Republic of Singapore Air Force received 12 FGA.74s and four FR.74As (ex-RAF F.6s modified to Mk.9/10 standards) in 1970–71 after the nation had acquired independence. These equipped 140 and 141 Squadrons based at Tengah, within the island's Air Defence Command. Another eight former RAF F.4s and 14 F.6s were supplied in 1972–73 along with four T.75s and five T.75As in 1970 and 1972–73. Most single-seaters were equipped to carry AIM-9 Sidewinder air-to-air missiles.

Somalia

A quantity of Hunters, at least ten, were supplied to Somalia by Abu Dhabi in 1983 and used for approximately six years.

Sweden

The Svenska Flygvapnet ordered 120 F.50s (F.4s) with Avon 115s direct from Hawker, the type entering service as the J 34 with F 18 Wing at Södertörn in August 1955 (more powerful Avon 119s and 120s were fitted later). The objective was to fill an air-defence gap between the J 29 Tunnan and the forthcoming supersonic J 35 Draken, with Hunters operating as day interceptors against bombers flying at high altitude; later these aircraft were modified to carry Sidewinders. The Flygvapnet used Wings (or Flygflottilj) comprising three squadrons, 1, 2 and 3, and these were identified by a colour, red, blue and yellow, respectively, while the staff aircraft for a wing was marked with white. Sweden's F.50s sported dark green upper surfaces and sky blue undersides, and no example had a sawtooth leading-edge mainplane.

In October 1956 F 8 at Barkarby became the second wing to receive J 34s, keeping them until disbandment in spring 1961. F 8's Hunters then joined F 9 Wing at Säve in 1962, later moving to Ängelholm. With the arrival of the Draken, F 18 Wing's Hunters (then at Tullinge) also went to F 9 and to F 10 Wings at Säve, where they lasted until 1969. However, just 2 Squadron of F 10 Wing used

Swedish J 34 34016 arrived at F 18 Wing in 1956. (Tony Buttler)

the J 34, from 1963–1967. Most Swedish Hunters were scrapped, just four returning to Kingston for rebuild into Swiss T.68s. Sweden never bought the two-seater.

Flight trials began in 1958 using Hunter 34085 fitted with a Svenska Flygmotor afterburner as a J 34 B; this refit included small additional mid-fuselage dorsal intakes. The aircraft's time-to-height was reduced drastically, with just four minutes needed to reach 39,370ft (12,000m); rate of turn was improved, but the afterburner flamed out at 42,000ft (12,800m) and so could not contribute to reaching higher altitudes. The programme was abandoned, though, in part because of the engine's high fuel consumption.

Switzerland

The Schweizer Luftwaffe ordered 100 F.58s (F.6s) with an additional tail parachute and enlarged ammunition link containers. The first 12 were ex-RAF but the rest new-build, with deliveries between 1958–1960. A further order followed for 52 F.58As (F.4s, F.6s and GA.11s, and two T.7s, upgraded to Mk.9 standard) all delivered in 1971–75, in many cases in kit form for assembly at the Federal Aircraft Factory at Emmen. Most had provision to carry two AIM-9 Sidewinders on underwing pylons. Finally, eight T.68 trainers were delivered in 1974–75, half being modified RAF Mk.4s and the remainder ex-Swedish Mk.50s.

Their service was extensive and in 1990 the Hunter still equipped Fliegerstaffeln 2 at Ulrichen, 3 (Ambri), 5 and 9 (Raron), 7 (Interlaken), 15 (St Stephan), 20 (Mollis), 21 (Turtmann) and 22 (Ulrichen and St Stephan). Previously, Fliegerstaffeln 1, 4, 8, 11, 18 and 19 had also been equipped with Hunters and the airfield list included Dubendorf and Meiringen, with trainers based at Turtmann. And if their runways were unserviceable due to enemy action, these Hunters could also use adjacent motorways as improvised bases/runways. Hunter pilot training at emergency operational locations such as these, deep in the Alpine region of central Switzerland, took place twice a year to enable them to retreat to more secure positions in the event of invasion. They would be defended by anti-aircraft guns and surface-to-air missiles. The last in-service flight by a Swiss Hunter, in fact by F.58 J-4001, took place in December 1994.

Swiss Hunter F.58 J-4007 in Fliegerstaffeln 7 colours, photographed during an April 1989 training course. The scheme was apparently applied for just three days. (Key)

OVERSEAS AIR ARMS
PRODUCTION LIST

Hunter F.58 *Papyrus*, **Fliegerstaffel 15, Swiss Air Force, St Stephan, 1993.**

(Refurbished airframes mostly Kingston)

Abu Dhabi

FGA.76 (7) Serials 701–707

FR.76A (3) 708–710

T.77 (2) 711, 712

Belgium

F.4 (112) ID-1 to ID-64 (all assembled in Belgium except ID-1 from Kingston as pattern), ID-101 to ID-148

F.6 (144) IF-1 to IF-144 (Belgium and Holland manufacture)

Chile

FGA.71 (28 + 15) J-700 to J-714, J-724 to J-735, J-737, J-738, J-740 to J-754

FR.71A (3) J-715 to J-717

T.72 (7) J-718 to J-723, J-736

Denmark

F.51 (30 all Kingston-built airframes) E-401 to E-430 (first 21 originally 401–421)

T.53 (4) ET-271 to ET-274

India

F.56 (160 Kingston) BA201–BA360 (BA201–BA248 ex-RAF)

T.66 (22 Kingston) BS361–BS376, BS485–BS490

F.56A (53) A459–A494, A936–A943, A967–969, A1010–A1015

T.66D (12) S-570 to S-581

T.66E (5) S-1389 to S-1393

Iraq

F.6 (15) 394–398, 400–409

FGA.59 (24) 570–587, 628–633

FGA.59A (18) 657–661, 690–702

FGA.59B (4) 662–665

T.69 (6) 567 (G-APUX), 567–569, 626, 627

Jordan

F.6 (13) 700–711, 717

FR.10 (2) 853, 712

F.73/FGA.9 (16) 801–812, 825, 826, 814, 832

F.73A (13) 828–831, 840, 842–849

F.73B (3) 841, 850, 851

T.66A (1) 800 (G-APUX)

T.66B (3) 714, 716, 718

T.70 (2) 835, 836

Kenya

FGA.80 (4) 803–806

T.81 (1) 801

T.8C (1) 802

Kuwait

FGA.57 (4) 212–215

FGA.6/FGA.9 (2 and 1) 216, 217, 220

T.67 (4) 210, 211, 218, 219

Lebanon

FGA.70/FGA.9 (5 and 4) L-170 to L179

F.6 (6) L-280 to L-285 (first five originally L-180 to L-184)

T.66A (1) L-581 (G-APUX)

T.66C (3) Initially L-286 to L-288, later L-280 to L-282

Netherlands

F.4 (96 all Fokker) N-101 to N-196

F.6 (93 all Fokker) N-201 to N-293

T.7 (20 – first 10 Fokker, remainder Kingston; N-301 to N-320

Oman

FGA.73/73A/73B (35) 718–725, 815–817, 825–832, 840–854

T.66B (3) 800–802

T.67 (2) 803, 804

Peru

F.52 (16) 630–645

T.62 (1) 681

Qatar

FGA.78 (3) QA-10 to QA-12

T.79 (1) QA-13

Rhodesia/Zimbabwe

FGA.9/80 (25) – first 12 RRAF 116-127; later random four-digit numbers on all

T.7/81 (1) 1084

Saudi Arabia

F.60 (4) 60–601 to 60–604

T.70 (2) 70–616, 70–617

Singapore

FGA.74 (12) 501, 502, 505, 507–511, 513, 515, 518, 519

FR.74 (4) 503, 506, 512, 517

FR.74B (22) 520–527, 529, 530, 531, 533–535, 537–539, 541–543, 545, 546

T.75 (4) 500, 504, 514, 516

T.75A (5) 528, 532, 536, 540, 544

Somalia

FGA.76/76A (9?) CC-701 to CC-707, CC-709, CC-710

T.77 (1) CC-711

Sweden

F.50/J 34 (120 – first 24 Kingston, remainder Blackpool) 34001–34120

Switzerland

F.58 (100 all Kingston) J-4001 to J-4100

F.58A (52) J-4101 to J-4152

T.68 (8) J-4201 to J-4208

Chapter 7

Combat History
Into Action

RAF Hunter F.5s from 1 and 34 Squadrons were detached to Nicosia, Cyprus, as part of the support force for Britain's involvement in the Suez Campaign of autumn 1956. For 1 Squadron this excursion lasted from September 1 until just before Christmas, with 34 arriving in October. On 2 November 1956 these aircraft flew top-cover sorties over the Canal Zone to support Royal Navy ground-attack aircraft, but the Hunter's limited endurance restricted its time in the patrol area and it did not repeat this duty. Instead, the main task of the Hunters in this theatre became fighter defence for Cyprus in cooperation with French Mystère IVAs, as a counter to the Egyptian Air Force attacking the island with its Ilyushin Il-28 jet bombers.

Once again, the Hunter's range performance, especially regarding its ground-attack potential, was criticised strongly and the RAF became somewhat envious of French Republic F-84F long-range fighter-bombers, which could attack targets in Egypt directly from Cyprus. It was clear the Hunter was a vastly superior aircraft in the high-altitude interceptor role, having an infinitely better ceiling, climb and turn performance, but the need for the F.6 with its greater range become even more important.

Hunter FR.10 XE589/RC, of 1417 Flight RAF, in action during the Radfan Campaign. This sub-unit was formed in March 1963 from the fighter-recce element of 8 Squadron, and was re-absorbed into 8 Squadron proper in September 1967. (All Tony Buttler unless stated)

XK150/A of 8 Squadron pictured in the early 1960s, soon after its conversion to FGA.9 standard.

RAF Middle East

On 25 June 1961 the Iraqi Prime Minister declared that Kuwait was an integral part of Iraq. In response, Britain began to move forces into Kuwait to counter a possible surprise attack or invasion. Iraq had Hunter F.6s of its own, but the British build-up in July included the Hunters of 8 and 208 Squadrons, the limited hard-standing area at Kuwait's airport becoming full of fast jets. The crisis eventually passed, though, and the biggest problem for the Hunter units to overcome, after having maintained high readiness for more than a week, was the severe desert climate.

After the Kuwait emergency, late in 1961 Middle East Command's two FGA.9 squadrons were formed into a single tactical unit called the Khormaksar Wing. The two squadrons then operated on a rotational basis between Bahrain and Khormaksar, staying for a month on each visit; those at Bahrain

Hunter FGA.9 XF431/Q of the Khormaksar Strike Wing, wearing joint 8 and 43 Squadron markings.

as a counter to further threats against Kuwait, while the aircraft at Khormaksar covered Britain's commitments in the Western Aden Protectorate and in East Africa as a whole. Aden then became the Headquarters of the RAF's Middle East Command.

The first operations within this role came in January and February 1962 when Hunters (and Avro Shackletons) dropped 1,000lb (454kg) bombs and a very large number of 20lb (9.1kg) fragmentation bombs on dissident villages. In September 1962 the new Imam of the Yemen began a strong campaign of propaganda against the Federation of South Arabia, calling for tribes to rebel and overthrow the Federation. Relations between Yemen and both the Federation of South Arabia and the UK gradually deteriorated, and 43 Squadron moved to Khormaksar in March 1963. From October that year, in deterrent flights known as Flag Waves, two Hunters would fly over specified areas at heights above 1,500ft (457m), outside the range of small arms, but without making any attacks. This proved effective for a while.

Then in December 1963 a state of emergency was declared after the number of attacks by Yemen-backed dissidents in the Radfan area began to rise. For the first time, Hunters were used to make cannon and rocket attacks against these terrorists. In March 1964 the Army moved into the Radfan to begin Operation *Nutcracker*, with air support for the ground troops coming from, particularly, the Khormaksar Wing Hunters. Over a two-month period they flew more than 300 strike sorties and 100-plus reconnaissance missions as the enemy was slowly pushed back. Operating with the Khormaksar Wing Squadrons was 1417 Flight equipped with the FR.10, and these aircraft proved especially valuable because they could take detailed photos of targets in areas where the available maps were not always of the best quality.

The Radfan, an area of approximately 20 x 15 miles (32 x 24km), provided a stiff test for the Hunter. This was the dissident tribes' primary stronghold and lay some 35 miles (56km) to the north of Aden. It was rocky and had peaks rising above 6,000ft (1,829m), which were then split by deep and often sheer-sided wadis. These features could produce substantial turbulence and sudden alterations in the weather and wind conditions, which at times severely tested the flying skills of the Hunter pilots.

Armourers fit rocket rails to a 208 Squadron Hunter. The unit was based at Khormaksar, but here the aircraft is on detachment to Amman in Jordan. (Key)

These FGA.9s of the Khormaksar Strike Wing, again wearing joint 8/43 Squadron markings, patrol the area's hostile terrain. (Key)

The incursions increased still further and began to involve Yemeni helicopters, with MiG-17 fighters as escorts. In response to one such attack, on 28 March eight Hunters smashed a Harib fort just over the border in Yemen. During April 43 and 208 Squadrons flew a limited number of ground support sorties, and in May this was followed by a more systematic campaign to destroy targets as the ground offensive gathered momentum. Then, on 7 June the fighting in the Radfan reached its peak, literally, with a major assault against Jebel Huriyah, a 6,125ft (1,867m) high mountain that dominated the entire Radfan. All day, endless Hunter attacks and artillery fire brought heavy enemy casualties and in the end the Battle of Jebel Huriyah proved decisive. Afterwards the volume of air operations was reduced but, between 30 April and 30 June 1964, 43 and 208 Squadrons launched 2,500 rocket projectiles in 527 sorties. Offensive operations over the Radfan by Khormaksar Wing Hunters ended on 18 November.

This FGA.9, XF511/F of 208 Squadron, was photographed at Muharraq, Bahrain, in 1967 with the later style of unit decor. (K Prentice via Terry Panopalis)

One of the Hunter FR.10s of 1417(FR) Flight, based at Khormaksar, was XF429/KS seen here in mid-1967. (Key)

The Hunter's contribution had proved invaluable. The FGA.9 was reliable and highly manoeuvrable (having constantly to pull 7g over the Radfan) and it was an excellent weapons platform. The Aden cannon proved accurate and devastating against 'soft-skinned' targets, while the 3in (76mm) rocket projectile could deal with stone buildings such as forts and houses. Along with its regular recce work, including pre- and post-strike photography, the FR.10 was also used to drop leaflets prior to a strike. A big problem, however, was sand, which quickly abraded the Hunter's canopies and necessitated the frequent changing of windscreens.

In January 1966 the British government announced it was to withdraw its forces from South Arabia, which itself would be granted independence not later than 1968. But fierce fighting broke out between the rival factions wishing to take control of the region, while at the same time Yemen/Egypt-backed dissidents began to attack urban areas of Aden State. For some months from January onwards the Khormaksar Wing Hunters flew air-defence patrols along the border with Yemen, while also having to support further ground action in the Radfan. For example, on 28 August 1966 the Wing attacked and destroyed the enemy fort at Shurjan with rocket projectiles and 30mm ammunition.

Hunters of 208 Squadron taxi to the runway at Amman, Jordan, in a view that shows the hot conditions experienced by the groundcrews. (Key)

In September 1967 8 Squadron moved to Muharraq, while 1417 Flight was disbanded. However, 43 remained at Khormaksar and continued its ground-attack support sorties, the last of which took place on 9 November. The British withdrawal was covered by Royal Navy aircraft operating from the carrier HMS *Eagle* and this allowed 43 Squadron to be disbanded. However, 8 and 208 Squadrons continued as the Offensive Support Wing at Muharraq until 1971, when the final British withdrawal from the Arabian Gulf theatre was completed.

RAF Far East

Another 'event' that would bring RAF Hunters into action was the Indonesian Confrontation of 1962–63. In May 1961 Great Britain proposed a new federation that would embrace Malaya, Singapore, Sarawak, North Borneo and Brunei, but nearby Indonesia opposed this idea very strongly. Then in December 1962 there was a revolt in Brunei. British troops were flown into the area and on 13 December the Hunter FGA.9s of 20 Squadron (plus Canberras from 45 Squadron) were moved from Tengah to Labuan. The Hunters immediately made firing passes over captured buildings at Seria, and within a week this revolt had been repulsed. But it marked the start of four long years of continuous operations by British ground forces, against Indonesia's efforts to stop Sarawak and North Borneo (later known as Sabah) becoming part of the State of Malaysia.

In March 1963 Indonesian guerrillas started to make cross-border raids, and these were increased once the Federation of Malaysia had been formed in September. At selected times 20 Squadron's Hunters were deployed to Labuan and Kuching, while Indonesia announced it would employ air and naval forces to support the insurgents. There were instances of the Indonesian Air Force's older piston-powered F-51 Mustang fighters and B-25 Mitchell bombers infringing Malaysian airspace, but the real worry were the fast jets operated by Indonesia, MiG-17 fighters and Ilyushin Il-28 bombers. Consequently, the Hunters, and some Gloster Javelin FAW.9R night and all-weather fighters, began to fly low-level patrols along the Indonesian border. In fact, an Air Defence Identification Zone was established around the Sabah and Sarawak borders, which stretched 3 miles (5km) offshore. To police this, four 20 Squadron Hunters were sent to Labuan and four more to Kuching; each base also received two 60 Squadron Javelins, thereby ensuring all-weather air defence was available around the clock.

Left: A splendid study of Hunter FGA.9 XT695/K of 20 Squadron in 1967.

Below: FGA.9s of 208 Squadron on 26 February 1964. Note the earlier style of unit markings.

Another 208 Squadron aircraft, XE532/K, in 1966.

In a further escalation, in August 1964 Indonesian forces invaded the Malay Peninsula, and attacks were also made against Malaysian patrol vessels and other facilities. Once again, the Hunters switched to ground-attack mode and from 3 September 20 Squadron's aircraft used cannon and rockets to attack enemy paratroopers well concealed in jungle hideouts. After a few days this particular 'invasion' had been completely defeated with many casualties among the invaders, but further regular landings and other attacks by Indonesian forces continued until the end of March 1965. The effort needed to counter these threats placed 20 Squadron's aircraft in continuous operations either engaging ground forces, supporting friendly soldiers, or on other tasks such as coastal reconnaissance.

At the same time, more Indonesian ground forces would regularly cross the Kalimantan border and these jungle missions increased during 1965. In fact, this proved to be the main Indonesian thrust within Borneo, but here the RAF Hunter's involvement was rather limited. Indonesian activity along the Kalimantan border began to fall away during 1966, partly because Indonesia's leader Sukarno was coming under growing international pressure to end the ongoing confrontation. A peace treaty was finally signed between Malaysia and Indonesia on 11 August 1966.

Dutch activity

Some time earlier, but due to growing concerns over Indonesian intentions, in May 1960 the Netherlands Air Force's 322 Squadron and its Hunter F.4s were embarked on the carrier *Karel Doorman* and ferried to the island of Biak to provide air defence. However, in these tropical conditions the performance of the F.4 was found wanting, particularly so in its rate of climb. Consequently, the unit had F.6s delivered from December 1961. Skirmishes with Indonesian forces over sovereignty issues occurred in 1962, but a United Nations resolution prevented this situation from developing into full-scale hostilities.

Dutch Hunters found it difficult to handle the Indonesian operations because of the enormous flight distances involved. To mitigate this, some examples had additional pylons fitted under their outer wings to enable two more drop tanks to be carried, doubling the F.6's range at altitude from 210 miles to 410 miles (338km to 660km), while still leaving five minutes available for possible combat. In addition, from May 1962 the Hunters began to operate from other bases outside Biak as and when required. The last flights by 322 Squadron on Biak took place on 15 September 1962.

India/Pakistan

Disputes between these neighbouring countries during the 1960s meant the Hawker Hunter was heavily involved in frontline action, taking some losses. This fighting also brought the first occasions when the Hunter participated in what it was originally designed for, air-to-air combat (and in doing so it became the first British swept-wing jet fighter to be engaged in aerial fighting). However, the Indian Hunters' first action came during Operation *Vijay*, the Indian annexation of Goa in December 1961. Here, 27 Squadron's aircraft were used for strafing runs against airfields and other ground targets.

The Hunter made a substantial contribution to the Indo-Pakistan War of 1965. From August that year, Pakistan became increasingly aggressive in the region of the disputed border with Kashmir. This culminated in a full attack that started on 1 September, using heavy armour and with the support of Pakistan Air Force aircraft, specifically the F-86F Sabre. The two closest Indian Air Force Hunter units were 7 and 27 Squadrons based at Halwara, and the first of these flew its initial offensive sorties in this campaign on 6 September, losing three Hunters to Sabres but shooting down three of the latter. Two more Hunters were lost the next day, but they were also supporting the Indian Army offensive with repeated attacks against ground targets. For example, on 8 September four Hunters employed cannon and rockets to destroy an ammunition train at Raiwind, although another Hunter was brought down by anti-aircraft guns during this operation. Two more Hunters were destroyed on the ground at Halwara on 14 September, when Pakistani B-57 bombers attacked at night; on 16 September one Hunter and one Sabre were shot down during an air-to-air battle over Tarn Tarn, and 20 September brought the destruction of two more Hunters.

An Indian Air Force twin-seat Hunter, coded BA360, keeps company with its single-seat equivalent. (Key)

The serial of this Indian Hunter F.56 is not sufficiently clear to read, but it's a fine example of this air arm's camouflage and markings on the type.

This conflict, which in the end lasted for 23 days, revealed Pakistan's Sabres were, in some respects, superior to India's Hunters in air combat with the latter apparently losing at least ten against the British design's six Sabre victims. The F-86F Sabre benefited from having Sidewinder air-to-air missiles on board when the Hunter had to rely on just guns. The Sabre could also out-turn the Hunter and the latter did not have self-sealing fuel tanks, which made it an easier target to destroy because of the increased risk of fire. However, India's Hunters performed splendidly as ground attackers, at times carrying substantial war loads deep into enemy territory (an example here was an attack on the Pakistani air base at Sargodha). As the RAF's Hunter pilots had found, the type's 30mm cannon proved highly effective against soft targets and the rockets dealt easily with railway and road vehicles, but they were not quite so successful against enemy armour. A very high proportion of the Indian Hunter sorties were made against ground targets, with most of the remainder being combat air patrol sorties. In the end, however, there were just two occasions in which Hunters and Sabres fought air battles at high altitude.

Hostilities between India and Pakistan broke out again in December 1971, although this time the situation was different for India because it had to deal with an enemy on two flanks. On 4 December Indian Hunters from 7 Squadron again flew raids against targets in East Pakistan (Bangladesh) in response to pre-emptive strikes made earlier by Pakistan aircraft. Three Hunters were lost but these raids against airfields near Dacca were quite extensive; they included the destruction of a bridge that crossed the River Teesta and the shooting down of three Sabres. However, the situation in the west resulted in 7 Squadron moving to Hinton airbase on 6 December, and eight Indian Hunters were also sent to Nal airbase (that same day a Sabre was destroyed by an Indian Hunter). A Hunter fell to ground fire near Dacca on 11 December, and Indian Hunters from 14 Squadron hit army positions in the district of Dinajur on the 12th.

To help its forces in the east as Bangladesh was striving for independence, and in an attempt to split India's forces, the Pakistan Army opened another campaign against Kashmir and the Punjab in the west. The Pakistan Air Force's principal interceptors were now the supersonic Soviet Mikoyan MiG-19 (or rather the Chinese-built F-6 version) and the French Dassault Mirage III, but again India's Hunters proved vital in providing ground-attack support. Six Hunters were lost on 4–5 December in raids against various targets in West Pakistan, with just one falling to ground fire. The next day, raids against Pakistan air bases ensured the destruction of more Sabres, along with B-57 bombers, and then from 7 December the Hunters attacked transport, armour and troops but a Sabre brought down one Hunter. Two more Hunters succumbed to ground fire on 9 December. The next day brought very heavy fighting on the Munawar Tawi river, and a Hunter was destroyed on the ground at its Pathankot base by a Mirage strafing run. A Sabre and an F-6 were shot down on 15 December by Hunters over the Sind Desert.

On 17 December this bitter war was brought to a halt by a general ceasefire, India apparently having lost 22 Hunters during the conflict, including at least 11 shot down by enemy aircraft. It was evident that in air combat, Pakistan's supersonic fighters held a considerable edge over the by then elderly Hunter.

Arab-Israeli conflict

Two of the main protagonists in the wars between Israel and its Arab neighbours, Israel itself and Egypt, never acquired the Hunter, but examples flown by other nations were dragged into the fighting.

The first major face off was the Six-Day War of June 1967. Here, the Hunters that equipped the Iraqi Air Force played just a small part, but ten were destroyed on the ground, and another five in the air when Israeli aircraft made a surprise attack on Habbaniya airfield. Following this setback, Iraq's Hunters focused on patrolling their country's border, but during the conflict they destroyed a pair of Israeli Sud-Ouest Vautours and one Mirage III fighter.

The Royal Jordanian Air Force had lost a Hunter to a Mirage on 13 November 1966, when four examples tried to counter an Israeli assault on a Jordanian village. With the opening of the Six-Day War the air force was active for just a very short time period. On the first day, 5 June, four 1 Squadron Hunters hit an Israeli airstrip at Kefar Sirkin where they destroyed military vehicles and light aircraft. However, all four were then downed by Israeli Mirages on their return to Mafraq, and indeed most of Jordan's Hunter force was subsequently destroyed on the ground at both Amman and Mafraq. On 6 June another Israeli Mirage IIICJ shot down a Lebanese Air Force F.6 belonging to that air arm's 1 Squadron, with the result that Lebanon's aircraft were never again involved in the Six-Day War.

The second major conflict was the Yom Kippur War fought in October 1973. This time Iraq's Hunters were more active and flown to airbases in other Arab countries to provide support. Twelve aircraft from 1 (FR) Squadron were deployed to Egypt, but the unit lost three examples on 8 October and another three on the 10th, all shot down by Mirage IIICJs. Another ten went to al-Mazzah in Syria to fly escort for Sukhoi Su-7s on ground-attack duties. In the air, they met Israeli Super Mystères and A-4 Skyhawks but just one Hunter survived, the remainder becoming casualties during intense air-to-air combat or to ground-based anti-aircraft fire/missiles.

Following the 1982 Lebanon War, when Israel invaded the Lebanon in response to constant aggression and counter-attacks between Israel and the Palestine Liberation Organisation, Lebanon's Hunters went into action against Druze militia. However, a number were lost to ground fire or through accidents.

A Jordanian Hunter gets ready to make its delivery flight from the Hawker factory. (Hawker Aircraft)

An Iraqi FGA.59. Note the long-range drop tank and retracted airbrake.

Other air arms

Oman: During the Dhofar War in 1975, Oman experienced increasing incursions into its territory by the People's Front for the Liberation of Oman, a body backed by Yemen. In response, on 17 October the Omani Air Force began to attack guerrilla positions along the South Yemen border and within South Yemen itself, here using bombs and rockets to support ground forces. Prior to 21 November the air strike targets had included rebel hideouts in Hauf. The operations with Oman's Hunters lasted right through to 2 December, when the Dhofari insurgency finally came to an end after 13 years with the capture of the last guerrilla-held village at Dhalqut.

An undated view of a Rhodesian Air Force Hunter, R-1284, at Durban. However, the photo was taken after airframe re-numbering had started. (Key)

Rhodesia: After this country had stated its Unilateral Declaration of Independence from Britain in 1965, its Hunters began flying patrols early in 1966 along the border with Zambia. As a counter, RAF Gloster Javelins of 29 Squadron, based in Zambia, flew patrols on the other side of the border, but ironically both forces had to come under the authority of Rhodesian Air Traffic Control, since this body covered much of Zambian air space.

Later that year, Rhodesia's Hunters performed low-level attacks against Frelimo guerrillas in Mozambique, in support of the Portuguese government. From 1972 1 Squadron's Hunters were once again employed against guerrillas, this time attacking camps in Zambia. These latest operations continued until a ceasefire came into effect in December 1979.

Somalia: In the 1980s, Hunters belonging to the Somali Air Force were used against rebel groups opposed to the regime of Siad Barre. However, the air force ceased to operate with the fall of Barre's realm in 1991, and the onset of civil war.

XG296 of 229 OCU pictured at Khormaskar.

Chapter 8
Aerobatic Teams
Smoke On!

The Hawker Hunter was such a superb aircraft to fly that pilots quickly championed it as a stable aerobatic platform.

Indeed, at 1950s Farnborough shows there appeared to be swarms of Hunters, with individual examples demonstrating various weapons options. Unsurprisingly, the type proved to be an excellent mount for formation flying and those events also brought the first appearances of RAF aerobatic display teams. With substantial foreign orders for the aircraft, some overseas air arms also formed their own teams.

North Weald was home to these 111 Squadron Hunter F.4s at the time this photo was taken in 1956. (Key)

United Kingdom

Hunter formation aerobatics began in the UK. The first RAF display team, formed in 1955, came from 54 Squadron, which sent four Hunters (F.1s and 4s) to that year's Farnborough show in September. Subsequently this team was named the Black Knights, not from the colour of their aircraft but due to the pilot's black flying suits. The 1956 Farnborough ushered in a team of four F.4s from 43 Squadron, but in fact for that year (and in 1955) the RAF had two official Fighter Command formation aerobatic teams, with the second on both occasions being the Hunter F.4s of 111 Squadron. As an illustration of their burgeoning skills, in May 1956 'Treble-One' gave a performance at Bordeaux, France, where its complement of four aircraft at one stage made nine simultaneous sonic booms!

For 1957 111 Squadron, then equipped with Hunter F.6s, took over as the RAF's premier display team, though at that stage they were still to be called the Black Arrows and flew just five aircraft. The CO was Sqn Ldr Roger Topp and in due course their mounts were painted in a splendid black livery. However, it is understood that several black/yellow schemes were trialled before this final form was selected. One of those rejected was named 'Golden Arrow' by those aircraft spotters who saw and photographed what was an overall black scheme, with a large yellow arrow-headed stripe along the aircraft's fuselage.

The Black Arrows truly made their mark at the September 1958 Farnborough, when they executed a loop of 22 Hunters in formation, a world record which still stands today. *Flight* reported that to enable 'Treble-One' to get so many aircraft together for this history-making achievement, the number was made up with Hunters and pilots supplied by 1, 2, 19, 56 and 92 Squadrons, CFE and 229 OCU. Having completed their famous loop, the Black Arrows then performed (during the same display) the

The Black Knights of 54 Squadron at Farnborough in 1955. The Hunters are WW641, WT659 and two F.4s. These aircraft had red and blue wingtips, but later the leader's aircraft (then WW636/Q) acquired a yellow lightning flash on a blue tail and another Hunter (WT692/S) had a blue flash on a yellow tail. (Adrian Balch)

Right: The famous 22-aircraft loop is practised by 'Treble-One's', Black Arrows, after they had borrowed Hunters and pilots from several other units. (BAE Systems)

Below: The display Hunters of 43 Squadron in 1956: WT641/T, WT613/R and WT587/N. (Key)

world's first barrel roll made by 16 aircraft in formation. Sqn Ldr Peter Latham replaced Topp in late 1958, and for his two-year tenure in charge he expanded the Black Arrows to a nine-aircraft outfit. Having developed and perfected the art of aerobatic flying by big formations of jet fighters, 111's final Farnborough came in 1960 where it presented an 18-strong 'Pterodactyl Loop' and then manoeuvres with two teams of nine aircraft.

From black to blue

In 1961 'Treble-One' was replaced by Sqn Ldr Brian Mercer's 92 Squadron as Fighter Command's formation aerobatic squadron. Initially the team was to be called The Falcons, but *Flight* reported this title did 'not appear to have met with general favour'. Later the same magazine noted that the team, with its aircraft painted in a splendid royal blue scheme with white wingtips, had been nicknamed 'The Blue Diamonds' by a German newspaper and this stuck (the Black Arrows title was apparently coined by a French newspaper).

The first displays were made on Whit Monday, 1961, during shows held at Wattisham, Hucknall and Yeadon and the performance involved groups of nine, seven and five aircraft. The Blue Diamonds developed new manoeuvres and formations of their own with plenty of smoke and much use of aircraft breaking away at unexpected moments. By that year's Farnborough in September there was a new formation called the 'Diamond T', in which seven aircraft flying in line abreast (very difficult to do) and another nine in a diamond behind, would perform a complete loop. The routine also involved a 16-ship roll in one large diamond and other manoeuvres with four split sections of four aircraft. T.7s eventually formed part of the team along with the F.6s and the unit also flew displays in Europe. No 92 Squadron continued its formation flying during the 1963 season, but with new mounts, supersonic English Electric Lightnings.

During the 1960s the Royal Navy's Fleet Air Arm expressed a liking for 'humorous' names for its display teams as a counter to the RAF's preference for more 'gung-ho' monikers. De Havilland Sea Vixen teams were formed, called Fred's Five and Simon's Circus, and in the summer of 1965 the Rough Diamonds were formed by 738 NAS. This had four Hunter GA.11s (with a spare aircraft attached) and retained the standard FAA Hunter colour scheme of Extra Dark Sea Grey over

The five-ship Black Arrows team in 1957 or 1958. (Crown Copyright)

The 92 Squadron RAF Blue Diamonds perform a 16-aircraft loop. (Crown Copyright)

white, although the aeroplane flown by team boss Lt Cdr Christopher Comins had Day-Glo red painted on its nose, wingtips and spine.

The Rough Diamonds were disbanded in 1969, but in 1975 a second naval Hunter formation aerobatic team was formed, called the Blue Herons, and again with four GA.11s and with Herons a reference to HMS Heron, in other words Royal Naval Air Station Yeovilton. The team was unique in that all four of its pilots were civilians (working for Airwork Services), though each had military backgrounds (the blue part of the name reflected their previous RAF or Fleet Air Arm experience, with their uniforms traditionally light or dark blue). The Heron's debut display was made at the Yeovilton Air Day on 6 September 1975, and they stayed together performing at major UK shows right through until the end of the 1980 season (one-off performances were subsequently staged at the Yeovilton Air Days of 1984 and 1986).

RAF Germany

Initially, most Hunter squadrons within 2nd Tactical Air Force (2 TAF) in Germany had display teams of their own. These included 20, 26, 93, 112 and 118 Squadrons, and in 1956–57 these units took part in competitions held at the start of these seasons to establish an official aerobatics display team, and a solo display pilot. In 1956 93 Squadron commanded by Sqn Ldr Desmond Browne, won the team competition while 118 Squadron supplied the solo, and this combination represented the Command at air shows across six European countries. The same combination won again in 1957, 93 then under the command of Sqn Ldr H 'Taddy' Minnis, but this time with Hunter F.6s rather than the Mk.4s used during the previous year.

Left: No 92 Squadron's the Blue Diamonds were famous for performing a loop in the 'Diamond T' formation, with seven Hunters lined abreast and another nine forming a diamond. (Key Collection)

Below: XE532/L (nose only), XG232/G and then a line of Hunter F.6s, of the Blue Diamonds, pictured at Leconfield in June 1961. (Adrian Balch)

There was never an official name for 93's team, which preferred instead to use its squadron identity, but it did introduce new elements in its aerobatic performances. For example, just seconds after retracting the wheels after taking off, one notch of flap would be selected by all pilots and then held throughout the performance until the approach for landing. This gave them a quicker engine reaction and operation with higher revs, which provided the capability to perform a display within a smaller air space. In addition, the acquisition of higher-thrust F.6s in 1957 enabled 93 to take off together in a box formation and then, after clearing the runway, to pull up into a loop and roll off the top to make a low-level return pass over the runway.

The solo Hunter's aerobatics would include climbs, rolls and loops, horizontal and vertical figure-8s using Derry turns, a spectacular inverted break for landing, and at one point a sonic boom from 40,000ft (12,192m). The latter would involve the Hunter diving supersonically to stay ahead of the boom, after which the pilot could enter the display area at subsonic speed and 'beat the boom'; this was intended to make some spectators think that a Hunter could in fact go supersonic in level flight.

The 1957 Defence White Paper brought an end to 2 TAF display teams after the 1957 season. Afterwards, the Black Arrows and Blue Diamonds would visit RAF air days in Germany, and 14 Squadron fielded a four-ship F.6 team in 1960.

Above left: **A spectacular photo of Blue Diamonds Hunters in line abreast and climbing to perform a loop. (Adrian Balch)**

Above right: **Four Hunters from 93 Squadron and the solo aircraft from 118 Squadron (centre rear), who in 1956–57 represented 2nd Tactical Air Force at airshows across Europe. (Tony Buttler)**

Overseas air arms

Belgium: The F.6 was the mount used by the Red Devils (or Rode Duivels/Diables Rouges) aerobatic team first commanded by Maj Robert Bladt. The initially unnamed squad, part of 7 Fighter Wing, gave its first public performance at Valenciennes, France, on 12 June 1957. To begin with it flew in standard camouflage before, at Chievres in October 1959, it appeared in a nine-aircraft formation with the lower wings of each aircraft painted in Belgium's national colours (in this display they were accompanied by 16 F.6s in standard colours). Cost-cutting then reduced the team to just four bright-red Hunters in 1960 (with two additional spare aircraft) and this was when the name Red Devils was coined. They performed their last show on 23 June 1963.

Holland: Two Netherlands Air Force units created Hunter aerobatic teams. The first was 325 Squadron, which ran the 'Darling' display group in 1956–57. The second was 322 Squadron with a team formed in early 1958 on its new Hunter F.4s; it later went on to perform with the F.6.

India: The Thunderbolts aerobatic display group was formed in 1982, specifically for the Indian Air Force's Golden Jubilee. It used nine 20 Squadron F.56As painted spectacularly in dark blue and white. The Thunderbolts continued to display until they were disbanded in 1990.

Jordan: In 1964 the Royal Jordanian Air Force formed a nine-aircraft Hunter team called the Hashemite Diamonds and, as the largest and only nine-ship team ever formed in the Middle East, it performed its first show on 4 November. The Hashemite Diamonds continued their displays in 1965 under the command of Flt Lt Hameed Anwar, who was seconded from the Pakistan Air Force.

Peru: For Peru's Aviation Day on 23 September 1956, the air force produced a four-aircraft team called Los Cuatro Ases (The Four Aces), and one speciality that lasted right through until 1961 and its disbandment was to fly routines and to land in rhomboid (diamond) formation. The team was often accompanied by a separate solo display Hunter called El Pájaro Loco (The Crazy Bird).

A dazzling Hunter F.56 from the Indian Air Force's Thunderbolts team. (Key)

Sweden: In 1956 a Swedish Air Force aerobatic display team was formed by F 18 Wing with four and later five Mk.50 (J 34) fighters. This was called the Acro Hunters (derived from the English word 'acrobatic') and specialised in 'British-style' displays, with smooth transitions from one formation to another and manoeuvres at low speeds (rather than following the 'American school' with lots of high-speed passes, full power and plenty of noise). The Acro Hunters were led by Sven Lampell and were initially called the Lampell Team. After increasing to five aircraft, they too introduced an individual or solo machine to fill in around the main section's formation passes. The team's last public display was on 1 September 1962, then it disbanded and was replaced by the Acro Deltas, equipped with the double-delta-winged SAAB Draken.

A separate Hunter display group was formed by F 8 Wing in 1958, called the Dyrssen Team after its commander Maj Gerhard Dyrssen. In 1959 he was succeeded by Robert Gustavsson who, in 1962, became the last CO for the Acro Hunters. Then for the 1964 season just F 9 Wing established a third and final Swedish Hunter display squad called the Göta Blue Hunters. Another five-aircraft unit, its mounts carried no specific markings and were led by Karl-Henrik Lindespang.

Switzerland: Perhaps the most famous Hunter display team formed outside the UK was the Patrouille de Suisse, founded by the Swiss Air Force in August 1964, with four Hunters. It used the type continuously in its Alpine environment and abroad until 1994, when it transitioned to the Northrop F-5E (though two displays in 1968 had the team flying the Dassault Mirage). In 1970 it was expanded to a five-aircraft unit and then soon afterwards to six. The Patrouille de Suisse proved very popular on its regular visits to the Hunter's home country, particularly to the Royal International Air Tattoos held at Fairford, Gloucestershire.

The Swiss Air Force Patrouille de Suisse aerobatic display team. (Key)

COMPLETE HAWKER HUNTER PRODUCTION LIST

Rockets are salvoed by a 1 Squadron FGA.9 at Cowden North range, East Yorkshire, 1964. (Key)

Built in UK for British service

Hawker P.1081 Research Aircraft (converted from P.1052).

VX279 (1 – built at Kingston)

Hawker P.1067 Prototypes

WB188, WB195, WB202 (3 all built at Kingston)

Hawker P.1083 Prototype

WN470 (1 – Kingston; not completed)

Hawker P.1099 (F.6 Prototype)

XF833 (1 from Kingston)

Hawker P.1101 Two-Seat Prototypes

XJ615, XJ627 (2 both Kingston)

Hunter F.1

WT555–WT595, WT611–WT660, WT679–WT700 (113 all Kingston); WW599–WW610, WW632–WW645 (26 all built at Blackpool)

F.2

WN888–WN921, WN943–WN953 (45 all built by Armstrong Whitworth at Coventry)

F.3

WB188 (1 prototype modified for research and speed record at Kingston)

F.4

WT701–WT723, WT734–WT769, WT771–WT780, WT795–WT811, WV253–WV281, WV314–WV334, WV363–WV412, WW589–WW591 (189 all Kingston – WT770 direct to Sweden); WW646–WW665, XE657–XE689, XE702–XE718, XF289–XF324, XF357–XF370, XF932–XF953, XF967–XF999, XG341 and XG342 (177 all Blackpool)

F.5

WN954–WN992, WP101–-WP150 and WP179–WP194 (105 all Coventry)

F.6

WW592–WW598, XE526–XE561, XE579–XE628, XE643–XE656, XG127–XG137 (118 all Kingston); XG150–XG168 (19 all Armstrong Whitworth, Baginton, Coventry); XG169–XG172, XG185–XG211, XG225–XG239, XG251–XG274, XG289–XG298, XJ632–-XJ646, XJ673–XJ695, XJ712–XJ718, XK136–XK176, XK213–XK224 (178 all Kingston – XK157–XK176, XK213–XK224 = 32 completed as Mk.56 for India as BA201–BA232); XF373–XF389, XF414–XF463, XF495–XF527 (100 all Armstrong Whitworth Coventry)

T.7

XL563–XL579, XL583, XL586, XL587, XL591–XL597, XL600, XL601, XL605, XL609–XL623 (45 all Kingston)

T.8

XL580–XL582, XL584, XL585, XL598, XL599, XL602–XL604 (10 all Kingston)

Built in UK for overseas service

Denmark

F.51 (based on F.4)

E-401 to E-430 (30 all Kingston)

T.7

ET-271, ET-272 (2 both Kingston)

India

F.56 (based on F.6)

BA201–BA232, BA249–BA360 (160 of which 145 new build by Kingston)

BA233–BA248 ex-RAF machines, though BA239 (ex-XE600) rejected and new BA239 built by Hawker

T.66

BS361–BS376, BS485–BS490 (22 all Kingston)

Jordan

T.66B (based on P.1101 trainer)

714 (1 from Kingston)

Netherlands

T.7

N-301 to N-320 (20 all Kingston)

Sweden

F.50 (based on F.4 and in Sweden designated J 34)

34001–34024, (24 all Kingston – ex-WT770 became 34001); 34025–34120 (96 all Blackpool)

Switzerland

F.58 (based on F.6)

J-4013 to J-4100 (88 all Kingston – J-4001 to J-4012 ex-RAF machines sold unused)

Built overseas under license

Belgium

F.4

ID-1 to ID-64, ID-101 to ID-148 (112 all built by Avions Fairey/SABCA)

F.6

IF-1 to IF-144 (144 all built by Avions Fairey/SABCA)

Netherlands

F.4

N-101 to N-196 (96 all built by Fokker/Aviolanda)

F.6

N-201 to N-293 (93 all Fokker/Aviolanda)

Grand total new-build Hunter: 1,972

(Overseas conversions are detailed under their respective chapters.)

Hunter T.8C XF357/637/LM of 738 NAS, Lossiemouth, in 1962. (Key)

Other books you might like:

Historical Military Aircraft
Series, Vol. 15

Historical Military Aircraft
Series, Vol. 12

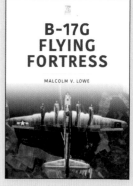

Historical Military Aircraft
Series, Vol. 11

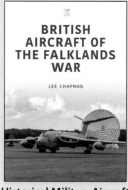

Historical Military Aircraft
Series, Vol. 13

For our full range of titles please visit:
shop.keypublishing.com/books